It's one thing to keep your kids focused on God during Christmas and Easter, but quite another to help them see the spiritual significance of Valentine's Day or Arbor Day. Bill and Penny Thrasher's book will help families think biblically about holidays throughout the calendar year.

JIM DALY
President, Focus on the Family

One of the most practical books ever on relationships and celebrating God's love through the holidays all year round. This book will draw you closer to Christ and to each other and help you celebrate milestones in meaningful ways. I highly recommend it.

CHRIS FABRY
Author and radio host

I love holidays! They are filled with family, fun, and an opportunity to step away from my "day job" for a change of pace. Yet sometimes our anticipation of the holiday outweighs the actual experience. For some, holidays are full of haunting memories of the past. So how do we make the best of holiday celebrations? Bill Thrasher has some helpful ideas that will take your holidays to the next level.

JOSEPH M. STOWELL
President, Cornerstone University

We often give but a passing nod toward traditional holidays without realizing that they were intended originally to be "holy days." This book will help put devotion on the agenda for our regular rhythms of life throughout the year, a sorely needed issue for many of us.

JOSH MOODY
Senior Pastor, College Church, Wheaton, Illinois

If you are concerned that the Christian holidays are becoming muted in the midst of the growing welter of state and national holidays—do not despair. Bill and Penny Thrasher's *Putting God Back in the Holidays* shows how you can better exalt Christ through the great days of the church calendar and, likewise, infuse the secular holidays with an elevating, life-giving spirit. What a positive read this is! And, because I know the Thrasher family, I can say that they live it out. Read this book and be encouraged and enriched.

R. KENT HUGHES
Senior Pastor Emeritus, College Church, Wheaton, Illinois

The Thrashers have written a very valuable book to help with holiday advice and direction. An important and timely read.

PAT WILLIAMS
Senior Vice President, Orlando Magic

Holidays are often endured, not enjoyed. While anticipated, the net outcome for families today is usually fatigue and frustration. Having navigated, often unsuccessfully, my family through the maze of holidays, I rejoice in this important work by Bill and Penny Thrasher. Any parents who wish to transform their holiday experience need to ponder their words carefully. They speak as practitioners, not theorists. They offer encouragement, not judgment. May you find refreshment in this book!

PAUL NYQUIST
President, Moody Bible Institute

Holidays are some of the busiest times of the year. It is so easy to get caught up in the details of preparing for the events surrounding the holiday. Bill and Penny show how each holiday can have spiritual significance for the body of Christ as well as each of us individually. Then they give us practical ways we can glorify God through the holidays and be conforming ourselves to the image of His dear Son.

MIKE SMITH
President, Home School Legal Defense Association

# Putting God
# Back *in the* Holidays

Celebrate Christmas, Thanksgiving, Easter,
Birthdays, and 12 Other Special Occasions with Purpose

## Bill & Penny Thrasher

**MOODY PUBLISHERS**
CHICAGO

All Scripture quotations, unless otherwise indicated, are taken from the *New American Standard Bible®*, copyright © 1960, 1962, 1963, 1968, 1971, 1972, 1973, 1975, 1977, 1995 by The Lockman Foundation. Used by permission. (www.Lockman.org)

Scripture quotations marked NLT are taken from the *Holy Bible, New Living Translation,* copyright © 1996, 2004. Used by permission of Tyndale House Publishers, Inc., Wheaton Illinois 60189, U.S.A. All rights reserved.

Edited by Pam Pugh
Interior Design: Ragont Design
Cover Design: Dog Eared Design
Cover Image: iStock, 123RF and Kirk DouPonce

Library of Congress Cataloging-in-Publication Data

Thrasher, Bill
Putting God back in the holidays : celebrating Christmas, Thanksgiving, Easter, Birthdays, and 12 other special occasions with purpose / Bill Thrasher and Penny Thrasher.
   p. cm.
ISBN 978-0-8024-8674-5
1. Holidays—Religious aspects. I. Thrasher, Penny. II. Title.
GT3930.T49 2010
394.265—dc22

2010017749

We hope you enjoy this book from Moody Publishers. Our goal is to provide high-quality, thought-provoking books and products that connect truth to your real needs and challenges. For more information on other books and products written and produced from a biblical perspective, go to www.moodypublishers.com or write to:

Moody Publishers
820 N. LaSalle Boulevard
Chicago, IL 60610

1 3 5 7 9 10 8 6 4 2

*Printed in the United States of America*

*Dedicated to our merciful God who knows how to meet each one of us in our darkest moments as well as our brightest; and to our precious family, extended family, and friends with whom we have had the privilege to spend our holidays; and to God's people with a sincere prayer that they will feel both understood in their struggles and aided in their celebrations of the holidays.*

# Contents

# Foreword

Every culture has holidays. These are days set apart to celebrate religious or historical events that are significant to the individuals who live in that particular culture. It is the nature of humans to remember and celebrate significant events. I believe that is because we are made in the image of God, and God is big on celebration. The Old Testament is filled with instructions from God on how the people of Israel were to celebrate certain historical events and certain spiritual realities. In the New Testament, Jesus entered into religious and cultural celebrations, including weddings. He instituted a special celebration for His followers focusing on the importance of His sacrificial death, which made possible our salvation.

Throughout history, individual Christians have differed on how, when, and whether or not to celebrate cultural holidays. There is certainly room for disagreement. I have chosen to recognize that we are citizens of two kingdoms. The spiritual kingdom is moving us toward an eternal time of celebration in the presence of God Himself, which will be like nothing we have ever known on earth. Our celebrations of religious holidays are designed to reflect that eternal celebration. We are also citizens of an earthly kingdom and have the opportunity to be light in the midst of darkness. I believe that cultural holidays give us an opportunity to reflect the light that we have received from God. In so doing, we may be God's instrument in bringing men, women, and children to experience the forgiveness and eternal life that Christ came to offer. To withdraw from these holidays is to miss this spiritual opportunity.

Bill Thrasher has selected a variety of religious and cultural holidays and has in this volume given us practical ways to celebrate in a Christ-honoring manner. This is a book that is long overdue, and I am grateful for the time and energy that Bill and his wife, Penny, have put into its preparation. It is my prayer that this book will help many Christians do what they sincerely desire to do: take every opportunity to receive and reflect the love of Christ to family and friends.

GARY CHAPMAN, PHD
Author of *The Five Love Languages*
and *Love as a Way of Life*

# Let's Get Started:
## *What's the Problem?*

For many of us, the problem of the holidays is not only physical—fatigue, too much to do, expectations, money—but also mental, emotional, and spiritual. A "joyous" time of year such as Christmas, for example, can be one of great struggle and depression. In fact, more suicides occur during that time of year than any other. I have talked to one friend whose holiday memories are filled with the pain of seeing his father drunk and, as a result, treating his family with violence. Another family friend bears the pain of many Christmases feeling abandoned as her daddy would leave the home and go off with another woman each holiday.

Is there a special spiritual battle around certain holidays? I have certainly asked the Lord that question, and these are some of the insights I have discovered. One factor is when a society celebrates Christmas, Thanksgiving, or Easter, attention is being drawn to Christ in a materialistic way—but still there is some acknowledgment of Christ's birth, death, and resurrection. There is an enemy who so hates the name of Christ that he no doubt targets those who truly represent Christ in this world. He also seeks to hinder all who have been re-created by Christ in any destructive way he can.

When I also began to realize how tired and exhausted I was as I entered most holidays, I gained another insight. For many, the myriad of our family, work, and church obligations during these times deplete physical, emotional, and mental energy. Any time our spiritual batteries need recharging can be a vulnerable season for us. It is often a struggle to stay alert to the Lord and make these spiritually meaningful celebrations.

It took time for me to also realize the unconscious expectations inside my soul with which I entered holiday times. After working hard to finish up teaching for a semester and preparing for a new semester, I had this attitude in my heart—"I deserve a break." Such expectations set the stage for conflicts because of the demands and expectations that were placed on me that, in my own mind, hindered my desire for rest.

These times can also be the reminder of many unfulfilled dreams. Observing traditions can be a painful reminder of a loved one who is no longer living. For some it is the memory of difficult circumstances that have created divisions in the family and have separated you from the unified family for which you had always longed. One godly girl openly expressed to us how painful it was to observe the joy of a Christ-centered, loving home as it contrasted with her home, which had been ravaged by divorce. For others it is pressure from cultural expectations to mark holidays in such secular ways that Christ is almost an afterthought. And for many, it is expectations from our children or even from our spouse who celebrated holidays differently while growing up than we did!

These spiritual pressures are also the setting for God's people to truly rejoice in the gift of Christ! He left heaven to live a humble life in a troubled world and to give *hope, peace,* and *love* to those who look to Him. Realize the spiritual pressures in your life and talk openly and candidly to Him about them. It is one of the most important ways to celebrate any holiday. As you rejoice in your blessing, intercede for the hurts and pains of others for whom the Lord leads you to pray.

Penny and I do not want you to feel pressure to follow every suggestion. You may come from a home that was indifferent or even hostile to the Lord, or you may come from a strong Christian heritage. You may be happily married, or in a difficult marriage. You may have gone through the pain of divorce, or you may not have ever married. You may be a single parent, or you may have a spouse who just doesn't have the time or interest to work with you to make holidays meaningful.

If in some way you feel understood in your struggles and are aided in your holiday celebrations to bring greater glory to Christ, our aim has been accomplished. It will be a privilege to pray for the readers of this book that you will have holidays that are truly blessed by God and that you will find holy pleasure in the most wonderful Person of all: the Lord Jesus Christ.

## PENNY'S Thoughts

What a surprise our first Christmas was to me as a newlywed! While I was eagerly anticipating my side of the family gathering and also welcoming friends who needed somewhere to go, Bill was anticipating rest, quiet, and no scheduled activities. It was difficult for me to understand his need for retreat and rest when my Christmases had been such joyous, people-filled, spiritual gatherings. As I look back, I see how God was asking us both to lay down our expectations and to seek His leading together for our holidays.

Some helpful questions to ask might be:

1. Lord, what are Your priorities for us this holiday?
2. What ministry are You entrusting to us this season?
3. Would You please keep us flexible enough to listen to You and Your leading?

# Section One
## *New Years*

Chapter
One

Celebrating a
*New Year*

As you read the Bible you will observe in the Old Testament the principles of giving the "first fruits" to the Lord.

*Honor the Lord from your wealth*
*And from the first of all your produce;*
*So your barns will be filled with plenty*
*And your vats will overflow with new wine.*
—PROVERBS 3:9–10

I once heard a Christian leader share how he had taken this principle and applied it to his time. He showed how as he gave the first few minutes of the day, the first day of the week, and the first part of the year to the Lord, he had experienced great blessing. His words certainly got my attention, and I began to ponder how I might apply them to my life. Though I was already making some attempt to give the first few minutes of each day and the first day of the week to the Lord, I had never thought about giving the first few days of the year to the Lord. On that April evening, I made a notation on my daily planner in the next year's January to give the first few days to the Lord.

## THE GIFT OF DAYS

When January arrived I found myself worn out. However, as a professor in a college I had a few days before my classes began, and I told the Lord that I desired to present the days to Him for His purposes. Of course this should be true of any day, but in these few days I was able to be more available to Him.

As I sought the Lord a few ideas came into my mind. One was to go through my belongings and give away clothes and other things that I had not used in a few years. This enabled me to begin the New Year with a uncluttered apartment. As I looked through some past journals written during the last few years, three things began to surface. Then the idea came to me to let these be my key three prayer requests for that year. These three prayer requests became the framework for the goals I set for that year. (See Practical Help 2, page 24.)

How can one get started setting goals? The apostle Paul referred to his salvation experience as having been "laid hold of by Christ Jesus." He described his pursuit of God's plan for him as to "lay hold of that for which also I was laid hold of by Christ Jesus" (Philippians 3:12). The idea is that when God saves an individual, He has on His heart a plan for him. Goal setting is not to be an exercise of planning out "our" dreams, but rather laying hold of the dreams that God has put in our minds and hearts as we delight in Him. The achievement of this is referred to as a "prize" that one is to pursue with all their heart (verse 14).

## WORTHWHILE RESOLUTIONS

Take out a sheet of paper and on the top of it write this question: "God, what do You desire me to trust You for in regard to my life?" This is the starting place for your goals. It does not need to be completed in one sitting. Keep it before you and trust God to make it clearer as you seek Him day by day. Ask Him to both clarify it and confirm it.

At the beginning of each year, trust God for goals during the year that will aid you in fulfilling your life goals. I have found it helpful to use these categories (see Practical Help 1, page 22):

### GOALS

- Spiritual
- Relational
- Financial
- Intellectual
- Recreational
- Vocational
- Physical
- Family

You should not necessarily feel compelled to use all these categories, and you may find it helpful to add others. These goals are to aid you in staying on course to fulfill God's will.

Andrew Murray speaks of three stages in the Christian life. The first stage is characterized by making resolutions and determining to keep them in *your* strength. The failure that comes from this leads to the second stage of the Christian life. The first stage of "I can do it" is replaced by "I can't" —when you feel that setting goals will only lead to failure and defeat. The third stage is characterized by the attitude of "I can't, but I must and I am going to trust God to do it."

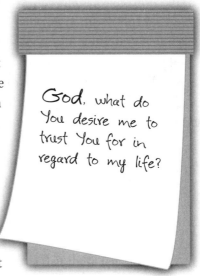

God, what do You desire me to trust You for in regard to my life?

It is in the spirit of the third stage that one finds freedom in setting goals. Therefore, I state my aspiration for the New Year in prayers and dependence on God. I have sought God for the past twenty-five years to give me three key prayer requests for the year. These three prayers set the foundation for any other goal for the year.

## LOVE AS THE FOUNDATION

The first year I did this I came to grips with the importance of love.

> If I speak with the tongues of men and of angels, but do not have love, I have become a noisy gong or a clanging cymbal. If I have the gift of prophecy, and know all mysteries and all knowledge; and if I have all faith, so as to remove mountains, but do not have love, I am nothing. And if I give all my possessions to feed the poor, and if I surrender my body to be burned, but do not have love, it profits me nothing. (1 Corinthians 13:1–3)

Whatever love was, I could not help but conclude that it was unquestionably preeminent. I also noted the truth of 1 John 4:19: "We love, because He first loved us."

If love was the most important thing in life, and if my love for God and others is only a response to His love for me, then I sensed what I needed to trust God for that year—"Lord, overwhelm me with Your love for me."

How do you know if you are overwhelmed with love? It is when you sense that He loves you in a way that no one else ever will or can. It is coming to grips with the truth that you desire and need One to love you who cannot get His mind off you. Listen to Psalm 139:17–18:

*How precious also are Your thoughts to me, O God!*
*How vast is the sum of them!*
*If I should count them, they would outnumber the sand*
*When I awake, I am still with You.*

God is constantly thinking about you!

This familiar passage opened up to me. Even Romans 5:5–10 took on new meaning one summer day that year when emotionally I was feeling ungodly. God set His love upon us when we were ungodly, helpless, sinners, and His enemies. These are not only verses to share with the unsaved but also to digest each day as a Christian!

Every time I saw a verse that encouraged me to love, I began to step back and ask God to show me how He loved me that way first. Remember, "We love because He first loved us" (1 John 4:19). For example, God tells us that a "friend loves at all times" (Proverbs 17:17). I would respond, "Lord, I know You desire me to be that kind of friend, but first help me to digest that You are that kind of friend to me!"

Include in your plan seeking the Lord and asking Him what He desires to do in and through you that year.

Verse 9 of Proverbs 17 tells us that while repeating past failure is one way to separate intimate friends, forgiveness is a way of seeking to build a relationship of love. This is what God desires for us in our human relationships with each other, and it is based on what He does for us. In our relationship with Him, what would it be like if every time you awakened, God reminded you of every failure you have ever done? That is not how He treats His children because He is seeking to build a loving relationship with them! These are some of the insights God gave me in response to trusting Him that year with the prayer "Overwhelm me with Your love."

How can you celebrate each New Year? Include in your plan seeking the Lord and asking Him what He desires to do in and through you that year. Then trust him to do it (see Practical Help 2 for an example of some of my past years' prayer requests)! Remember that He is a living God and He responds to the humble prayers of His people. We will talk more about goals in the next chapter.

## PENNY'S Thoughts

We have friends down the block who followed the leading of the Lord and hosted a gathering with friends to seek Him together as they welcomed the New Year. What a great idea! Here is their invitation:

### NEW YEAR'S PRAYER AND PRAISE

But you, dear friends, devote yourselves to prayer, keeping alert in it with an attitude of thanksgiving. And pray in the Spirit on all occasions, with all kinds of prayers and requests . . . building yourselves up in your most holy faith. Colossians 4:2; Ephesians 6:18; Jude 1:20

The occasion was held on the evening of December 31 starting around nine o'clock and going until midnight. In this case, families left their children with babysitters so the adults could

*Include in your plan seeking the Lord and asking Him what He desires to do in and through you that year.*

spend time praying in the New Year. You might want to hire child care in the home of the host; whatever works for your situation.

After a time of refreshments, the host led out, following the ACTS model of prayer. This model is practical for both personal and corporate prayer, and is adaptable for all ages. That time was so special that the guests wanted to do it again the next year!

**ACTS:**

**A**—adoration. Praise God for who He is; His name, attributes, character. If desired, sing hymns of praise and adoration.

**C**—confession. Humble yourselves before God, confessing any known sins and asking His Holy Spirit to reveal sin you might not be aware of.

**T**—thanksgiving. Look over the past year and thank God for answers to prayer, specific blessings, and so on.

**S**—supplication. This is the time in your prayer to make your requests according to His Word. For New Year's especially, you might direct prayer toward the salvation of family, friends, coworkers; personal spiritual growth; the universal church; the persecuted church; our nation and its leaders; ministry in our homes, workplaces, neighborhoods.

## PRACTICAL Help 1
### Holiday Prayers and Goals for a New Year

This is a sheet I pass out to my family members as an encouragement for each of us to put down our goals for the New Year.

These are six possible things to trust God for during the holidays and the coming year.

I. Trust Jesus to enhance your relationship with Him.
2. Trust Jesus to give you rest and refresh you.
3. Trust Jesus to show you how to be a vessel of love.
4. Trust Jesus to keep a measure of discipline in your life.
5. Trust Jesus to prepare you for any special temptations.
6. Trust Jesus to give you His goals for the New Year.

Here is an example of how you might pray:

"Dear Lord, during this year I ask that You show me how to be a vessel of Your love. Develop my character so I reflect Your love. Show me where I need to reach out, perhaps to neighbors who may need kindness." [for children: "Help me be a friend to ____ at school/church. Sometimes the kids make fun of him/her and it's hard for me to be nice. Please help me and help ____ know You love him/her."]

"Lord, You know that I've been critical of my boss. I am often tempted to talk about him to my coworkers, and I usually give in to this temptation. Keep the goal before me of being alert when I am tempted and to call on You to resist." [for children: "Dear God, help me not join in when kids are making fun of our teacher."]

Consider goals in some of these or other areas; here are a few examples to get you started, though your list might look very different!

**SPIRITUAL LIFE:** memorize ten new verses of Scripture; invite a particular friend or neighbor to an event at church; follow a Bible-reading plan

**RELATIONSHIPS:** cultivate existing ones and reach out to make new ones; be intentional about spending time alone with each child

**PHYSICAL/CARE FOR BODY:** walk three times a week

**INTELLECTUAL GROWTH:** read ten books during the year

**FINANCES:** make a budget and evaluate purchases each month

**RECREATION:** sign up for a _____ class with _____

**VOCATION:** attend a conference; learn a new technique

**SCHOOL/ACADEMICS:** finish homework before leisure time

**OUTREACH:** sign up to be a pen pal to someone in prison

**OTHER:**

# PRACTICAL HELP 2
## Examples of First-of-Year Prayer Requests

(These are some of the request that I have prayed over the years. Choose a few that are most meaningful to you. You may want to adapt these for your children, depending on their maturity levels.)

- Overwhelm me with Your love so that I can respond by more fully loving You (I John 4:19).
- Open my eyes to see the beauty of Your character in a way that wins my complete heart to You.
- Restore me to my first-love relationship with You (Revelation 2:4).
- Teach me what it means that all things belong to me in Christ (I Corinthians 3:21–23).
- Free me from any unhealthy compulsions.
- Teach me both the obstacles and the refreshing insights that lead to true joy.
- Enable me to love with *Your* light load and reject all false burdens that lead to a false compassion.

- Show me how and when to benefit from the discipline of silence.
- Open my eyes to see Your adequacy and generosity.
- May my imagination be fully presented to Your control.
- Overwhelm me with Your mercy.
- Deliver me from my fears by letting me seek God at every point of fear (Psalm 34:4).
- May my eating, exercises, and dress be under Your control.
- Show me how I fail to enjoy the grace of God in the Christian life.
- Teach me Spirit-led praise in my life.
- Guide me in processing all unrighteous anger in my life.
- Build a godly contentment, humility, and fear of You in my life.
- Teach me to enjoy life to the glory of God.
- Lead me into a refreshing and encouraging intimacy with You and Your people.
- Give me an eternal perspective that grasps the reality of heaven and hell and my role as a pilgrim on this earth.
- Show me how to be used by You to raise up prayer among Your people.
- Give me wisdom to understand my role and responsibility as a parent.
- Give me wisdom to have a healthy view of myself.
- Develop in me a Spirit-led initiative and deliver me from an unscriptural passivity that causes me to be influenced in ungodly ways.
- Flood my heart with a knowledge of Your acceptance and understanding.
- Develop in me a fear of God.
- Develop in me a heart of praise.
- Give me godly ambitions for eternal things.

- Show me how to devote myself to refreshing prayer and love the world through my prayers.

- Show me how to honor You by using Your Sabbath principle.

- Guide me to fully obeying You in seeking to win the hearts of my family to the Lord.

- Develop in me the heart of a "Mary" who knows how to enjoy You and live in peace (Luke 10:38–42).

- Put in me a trust in Your sovereignty in my life.

- Let me give You the firstfruits of my money and my time.

- Let me remember the truth that I walk with an all-powerful God each day.

- Put in me a trust in regard to the results of all ministry efforts (Mark 4:26–29).

- Build in me a heart of worship, to love, fear, and seek God.

- Enable me to fulfill my vows to You.

- Build the sense of responsibility in me and my family and grace us with the capabilities to do our responsibilities.

- Put in my heart an awe of You that leads to an intimacy with You.

- Teach me and my sons what it means to be a man and prepare us for all that it is to lead.

- May I be emotionally focused on Christ and not an idol.

- Give me the time alone I need to stay refreshed in You.

- Give me an understanding of what it means to live under grace and let me display this to my loved ones.

Chapter
Two

Setting Goals
*for the*
*New Year*

If you have not taken out a sheet of paper and written on the top of it the question, "Lord, what do You desire for my life?", plan when you will do so. If all you do is to simply write the question, it is a start. As you live life before the Lord, be open to conversations, experiences, and insights from Scripture that will prompt thoughts that will help you clarify your deepest heart longings. Commit these to the Lord in prayer and trust Him with them. "He is able to guard" what we entrust to Him (2 Timothy 1:12).

I try to take two days a year to devote to trusting God to confirm my life direction. I may not always be able to clear myself from all other responsibilities on these days, but I do trust the Lord to confirm the direction of my life and adjust any pursuits that need to be omitted or added. At the end of the day I write down any thought that I desire to record for further reflection.

One year, at the end of a summer that, at best, would be evaluated as mediocre in regard to my relationship to the Lord, I looked at the papers where I had written down what I was trusting God for in my life. As I read it I came to two conclusions. One was that my life goal was not as clear to me as I thought it was, and secondly I was not as committed to it as I thought. I rewrote all that I had written, and it was at that time that I began to take two days a year—one in December and one in May—to trust God to confirm and adjust my life direction.

## TOO MUCH INFO?

My life vision is due in large part to a prayer that God did not answer. I earnestly prayed for God to show me His plan for my whole life. I told Him that if He would allow me to envision my future work, I would use all my schooling to consciously prepare for it. It seemed to me that God had given Hudson Taylor a clear vision to work in China, which enabled him to diligently prepare for this work while still living in his homeland of England. I cried to God for this, but He never gave it. As I shared this experience with a pastor I was working with, he replied, "You are the kind of person that if

God gave you that, you would miss out on the present in thinking about the future."

## THE TRUE GOAL

John Wesley instructed his followers, "Don't seek for a ministry but anticipate the fruit of a disciplined life." If God had given me as clear a vision of what He wanted me to *do*, as I desired, I would have missed out on the developmental aspects of God's will for me—what He wanted me to *become.*

In regard to your vision and desires for your life, start with the discipline of Scripture. It is unquestionably His will for His words to abide in you (John 15:7) and for you to be set apart by His truth (17:17). If this is clearly your *life* goal, your celebration of each new year would include some sort of plan for getting His Word into your life. As you take time to seek confirmations for your goals, you may need to be reminded that the discipline of getting Scripture in your life is not an end in itself—it is a means to the end of increasing knowledge of Christ. This is what the Lord reminded a group of religious leaders one day: "You search the Scriptures because you think that in them you have eternal life; it is these that testify about Me" (John 5:39).

*He will unfold your life calling, and give you prayer burdens and goals each year that work toward its fulfillment.*

As long as you keep this end in mind, ask God to give you an unquenchable appetite for His word. The overflow of your relationship with God will be the foundation of whatever He calls you to do. One of the directions that have come from these special days has been to take some time out to write each day. (See

Practical Help 3 on page 32 for other ideas.) These special days have helped to clarify God's calling for my life.

All of this is very much within your grasp as you take the principle of firstfruits and apply it to your time. As you celebrate each day and each year with this principle, expect God to do above and beyond all you could ask and think (Ephesians 3:20). He will unfold your life calling, and give you prayer burdens and goals each year that work toward its fulfillment. Through the years you will be given scriptural convictions that will give direction to your life. The result will be both a vision for your life and the tasks to fulfill it. As someone has said, "A vision without a task makes a visionary, and a task without a vision is drudgery." However, a vision and tasks to live it out produces a missionary. In His will and timing God desires to give you both.

## PENNY'S Thoughts

How do we do this in our family? Last year, while driving down to Alabama, Bill gave us each our sheet (Practical Help 1, page 22) and asked us to prayerfully write out what goals we thought God would have us make. Later we went around and shared our goals while encouraging one another with supportive words. My mother joined in as well. We ended the time praying over the goals for one another. During the year Bill followed up with each son, asking them to review their goals and see if they were on track.

You might want to share your year's goals after supper one night. Or perhaps in your family, setting goals for a month at a time would be more doable. If you have school-age children, a goal under the Spiritual category could be to read a Bible passage or devotional each morning before or during breakfast. If your children need to spend more time in recreation and less with the computer, express that under Physical/Care for Body.

# PRACTICAL Help 3
## Examples of Convictions That Aid in Giving Life Direction

- Do not be distracted by activities and ministries that are not for me.

- Study and meditate daily on some verse or verses of Scripture (Acts 6:4).

- Let my fears, anxieties, anger, and all temptations drive me to prayer.

- Live out my calling as a teacher of God's Word to aid Your servants to apply truth to the depth of their being.

- Continually seek to progressively learn to walk by Your Spirit.

- Never say an unnecessary word behind another's back that puts them in a bad light or damages his or her reputation.

- Praise God's name daily and give Him the glory for every gift He gives.

- Give up all my personal aspirations that He may fill me with His aspirations.

- Seek to consciously and conspicuously experience His presence (Psalm 27:4).

- Let all my desires lead me to God (John 7:37–39).

- Trust God to rest and refresh me (Psalm 23:2).

- Seek to be blameless in love to the whole body of Christ (Philippians 1:9–11).

- Let Jeremiah 9:23–24 be the aim of my life.

- Continually believe God to work in my life the qualities of 2 Peter 1:5–7.

# Section Two
## *Birthdays*

Chapter
Three

# Celebrating
# *the Birthdays of*
# *Your Children*

Isaiah 41:10 is the verse that Penny was drawn to as she anticipated the birth of our first child. We had a godly midwife who
had encouraged both of us to seek God and ask Him to give us a
verse to which we could anchor our faith during the labor process.

Do not fear, for I am with you; Do not anxiously look about
you, for I am your God. I will strengthen you, surely I will
help you, Surely I will uphold you with My righteous right
hand.

How do we know when we can claim a verse that was not
written directly to us originally? When you interpret a verse, first
discern the original audience—in this case the nation of Israel.

Look at what you have in common with the original audience. Examine to see if the general teaching of Scripture would
deem the verse to be a general principle that is true for all of God's
people at all times. For example, God's promise to Abraham to
father the Jewish nation is true for only him and not all of God's
people. The Bible is to be read with integrity and with an alertness
to context. It is also to be read knowing that it is not only ancient
history but from a personal God who had every generation of His
people in mind when He inspired men to write Scripture.

For whatever was written in earlier times was written for
our instruction, so that through perseverance and the
encouragement of the Scriptures we might have hope.
(Romans 15:4)

## BIRTH DAYS

Isaiah 41:10 encouraged Penny. As her contractions began, I,
the nervous father, called the world asking for prayer only to discover that it was a false alarm. She was sick that night and could
not keep her food down. Her contractions really did begin at 6 p.m.
the next night, and she began the process with no food in her

system. Twenty-one hours later at 3:01 p.m. God called forth William Reynolds Thrasher into the world. God did calm our fears and gave strength until the very end.

Michael Scott came into the world about two and a half years later. His birth process lasted only six hours. My wife said that if it were fifteen minutes longer she could not have made it.

Five and a half years later I received a call from campus security one Tuesday night instructing me to rush home because my wife was in labor with our third child. I was teaching an evening class and giving an exam, but I raced home thirty miles only to discover that the contractions had stopped. As I arrived at school the next day and sat down at the faculty meeting, a staff member informed me again that my wife was in labor. I was told not to panic but to catch the next train and come home. I arrived home about two hours later and this time discovered that my wife's water had broken and the process was moving fast. I drove her to the hospital and just thirty minutes later God called forth David Preston.

We later learned that a baby boy who had been born just before David was had not made it to the hospital but was born in the car. His parents named him—this is a true story—**Car**son!

## BIRTH STORIES

One way to celebrate your children's birthday is to continually tell them their birth story. Birth is of God, and while it happens every day it is a miracle that a living person has been created! Telling their story is a way of reminding them and ourselves that they are a "gift of the Lord" (Psalm 127:3).

As I tell the story I recall the people who were with us at the birth like the nurse named Eloise whose humor got us through the intervals of the first birth. I tell them of my delight in God's design of them and the joy of holding them for the first time. I recall reading Psalm 23 to them and praying that our hearts would always be knitted together. I share the joy that they have brought to our family. It is a way to rejoice in God and affirm them as you celebrate their birthdays.

If your son or daughter was adopted, you can have a "When God blessed us with you" story. The same can be true for foster children who might be in the home as well.

*One idea I will pass along is a letter that I write to each one on his birthday.*

One other idea that I will pass along is a letter that I write to each one on his birthday. I begin it by calling him my beloved son and telling them that I am well pleased with him. The one Perfect Father affirmed His Son this way (Matthew 3:17); and we can remember that He loves His people with the same intensity as He loves His own Son. (See John 17:23.)

I have never given any of these letters to my sons, but when they leave home, eighteen plus letters in a folder will be given to them along with other things in a memory folder. You may choose to give your children a letter each year on their birthday. You might also invite other adults to write a short note—a coach, a music teacher, a youth group leader.

Your children are God's gifts. May God give you His wisdom in celebrating their birthdays in a way that honors Him and blesses them.

## PENNY'S Thoughts

Our three sons have enjoyed planning their birthday menu—breakfast, lunch, and dinner. With their stomachs being filled with their favorite food, it is a great time to feed their soul as well. Many times we have gone around the table sharing what character qualities we see and enjoy in them. We have shared special memories, baby books, or videos. Many times we go around the table asking God to bless them in specific ways in the coming year.

Chapter Four

Celebrating *Spiritual Birthdays*

William John Bauer was one of twenty thousand soldiers who boarded the Queen Elizabeth in New Jersey during a snowstorm to sail across the Atlantic in late January of 1945. Because there were only ten thousand beds, the soldiers alternated their sleeping patterns. One day during his waking hours, William entered a Bible study with twelve other soldiers on their voyage to Scotland. While he had gone to church and had heard the gospel, he had never taken it personally because he felt like he had plenty of time to make a decision. Six days later he arrived in Glasgow, Scotland, and began further training at an Air Force base.

William Bauer's assignment was to be a Ball Turret Bomber in a B17. He was also given three targets—the primary target, the secondary target, and the target of last resort. While flying over Frankfurt, Germany, their plane encountered heavy enemy artillery. During this moment he remembered the gospel message he had heard at the Bible study on the trip across the Atlantic and cried out to God. He prayed, "Lord, I have heard Your gospel many times and have always felt I have plenty of time, but *now* I am reaching out to You for Christ's gift of salvation." He later exclaimed, "God met me; I felt as if I could fly without the planes." The B17 miraculously made it back to land with three hundred holes in it from enemy artillery. They had also lost the brakes and one of the engines. He was miraculously spared physically and also saved spiritually on that fateful March 6, 1945.

## WILLIAM BAUER'S GRANDSONS

Fifty years later to the day—March 6, 1995—Michael Thrasher, his grandson, crawled into the bed with his mother and inquired how he could be saved from his sin and have a relationship with God. It was one of the most joyful telephone calls I have ever received when Michael called me at work and shared with me that he had trusted Christ.

Will, Michael's older brother, had been saved about three years earlier. One night, Will, almost four years old, was taking a bath with his one-year-old brother Michael. Michael went under the water and could not breathe. He was rescued, but the incident brought the reality of death close to home for Will. At that tender moment I had the privilege of leading him to the Lord on October 6—the day of my father's physical birth. When he was eleven he wrote a copy of his testimony that he shared at a nursing home. He called it his autobiography.

## MY AUTOBIOGRAPHY
### *by Will Thrasher*

Life. It's a precious thing. I'm talking about a different life called spiritual life. For Jesus said in John 4:13–14, "Everyone who drinks of this water will thirst again; but whoever drinks of the water that I will give him shall never thirst; but the water that I will give him will become in him a well of water springing up to eternal life." In other words, if you drink Jesus' water you will never thirst again. Here's the story of how I found the well of life.

In January of 1990 a blue-eyed big and burly boy entered the world, his name—Will Thrasher. I am privileged to be the first born of three boys. The second-born, Michael, is two and a half years younger and has been a fun-loving companion—but iron does sharpen iron!!!! Dear David is our youngest at age three and provides much humor in more ways than one!!!! My diligent and devoted dad is a professor at the Moody Bible Institute and, for much of my life, I traveled with him as he spoke in churches and retreats. My precious mom is a homemaker who is having a lot of fun juggling our homeschooling, music, and recreations. Even though I was born into a wonderful Christian family, that doesn't save me from sin; this is what did.

Even though I deeply enjoyed hearing the Bible read to me, I still didn't completely comprehend what being a Christian meant. One crispy fall October night in the bathtub, my brother Michael who was only one and a half years old at the time, slipped under the bathwater. Because he was so young, I knew he couldn't swim. I realized if my mom hadn't lifted him up, he would have drowned. Filling my mind were many questions about death, heaven, and hell that I spilled out to my dad. Daddy explained to me that Jesus Christ died on the cross, shedding His blood for my sins and the sins of everyone. All I had to do was believe on the Lord Jesus Christ. I eagerly accepted His free gift of salvation, and a flood of warmth poured over my body. My parents have since then nurtured me, and as they did, I began to understand more and more. How does being a Christian affect my life?

Believe me, I am not perfect, but I can turn to Jesus even when I have the most diminutive sins and He will blot them out. Jesus is my best friend. He fully helps me in all my problems and His constant presence is a comfort. I am now burdened for my little brother David's salvation. I long for his sins to be covered too!!!!!

Life. It is a precious thing. So precious in fact that we should lay down our lives that others might live. Jesus laid down His life for us. In fact, Scripture says, "Greater love has no one than this, that one lay down his life for his friends." Do you want to find the well of life? Are you troubled? Do you know for sure that you will spend eternity in God's glorious heaven? I would plead with you to accept the priceless offer of Jesus' blood as payment for your sin. May God usher you into His abundant life!

Will carried a great burden for his younger brother's salvation. His world was very small and to imagine an eternity without Michael was too much to handle. Crying himself to sleep he would pray for Michael's salvation and try to share the Lord with his younger brother. As Will preached verses on salvation to Michael, I heard him one time exclaim, "Michael, it is the Word of God!" Being his own man, Michael did not respond. In time God's Spirit convicted his little heart of his need for salvation fifty years after his grandfather had met the Lord in the air. Will had the joy of personally leading his youngest brother David to the Lord on a February 6. He wrote down a short poem about his brother for his English class.

*Will Thrasher*
*Mrs. Fisher*
*Fr. Eng. Hon, 7th period*
*14 April 2005*

*David. The joy*
*He brings to the life of*
*Me and my family.*
*His bright bubbling mischievous*
*Smile. The way he prays for*
*Me at night.*
*I love David.*

*Awesome athlete; stellar scholar; magnificent musician.*
*My brother is talented.*
*He hugs are filled with*
*Love. Words of encouragement pour from his mouth like a*
*Dreamsicle from a machine.*
*What would I do without Dave?*

*I would readily die for him.*
*Take my life in place of his.*
*Davie is a precious treasure;*
*Unique in every way.*
*I was privileged to lead him to the*
*Lord. That was the most gratifying moment of my*
*Life. There is no one like*
*David. That is why I love him.*

## "NEW BIRTH" DAYS

On February 6 (David), March 6 (Michael), and October 6 (Will) we have a spiritual birthday celebration. It is celebrating their new birth and even creating a thirst in the younger children to also have another birthday. The focus is on some opportunity for them to foster their spiritual growth. It has been the occasion to present them with the gift of their first Bible and also key books and videos that provide spiritual input.

*Spiritual birthday celebrations can be a time to confirm one's understanding of salvation.*

David began to have doubts about his early profession of faith. It was on November 18 after hearing a stirring sermon on Acts 7 and later watching *Amazing Grace* that he was greatly troubled about his soul. He cried tears of repentance that night in our bed for an hour. His spiritual birthday is now November 18. Last year on November 18 we watched a DVD of *Amazing Grace* and thanked God for his salvation.

Spiritual birthday celebrations can be a time to confirm one's understanding of salvation. Spiritual birthdays have also been a time for inviting people over to hear their testimonies. This has been followed by a time of discussion over a meal. I have invited both older men as well as some of my students to participate in this way.

This occasion can also be a time of giving to others in response to what God has so graciously given you. One spiritual birthday we took a young man, who was currently my student, out to eat. After listening to his testimony my son took time to pray for him and the salvation of his four-month-old baby.

It can also be celebrated with a spirit of mystery and adventure. One afternoon we blindfolded Will and put him in the car and picked up two of his friends. Driving downtown and arriving at a gushing fountain of water and removing his blindfold we quoted John 7:37–39:

> Now on the last day, the great day of the feast, Jesus stood and cried out, saying, "If anyone is thirsty, let him come to Me and drink. He who believes in Me, as the Scripture said, 'From his innermost being will flow rivers of living water.'" But this He spoke of the Spirit, whom those who believed in Him were to receive; for the Spirit was not yet given, because Jesus was not yet glorified.

We then went to a restaurant and purchased a milkshake for everybody.

A spiritual birthday celebration may be simply a time of togetherness and fun. As I was praying about how to celebrate Michael's spiritual birthday one year, a student came up to me and offered me two tickets to a Chicago Bull's game. I wrote down the gift on our "Jehovah Jireh" list. "Jehovah Jireh" is a name for God that means "the Lord will provide." In this case He "personalized His name" by providing a special time with my son with a courtside ticket to a professional basketball game at no charge.

God knows how to aid you in celebrating the spiritual birthdays in your family. If you do not know the day, simply pick a date on the calendar and begin celebrating each year. Your assurance of salvation is not based on knowing the date that you trusted Christ, but on simply knowing that your confidence is in Christ alone today to save you from your sin and His wrath and enable you to fully enjoy His peace and His love. If you have never had a spiritual birthday, there is no better time than today. Salvation is a gift of God.

For God so loved the world, that He gave His only begotten Son, that whoever believes in Him shall not perish, but have eternal life. (John 3:16)

For by grace you have been saved through faith; and that not of yourselves, it is the gift of God; not as a result of works, so that no one may boast. (Ephesians 2:8–9)

# PRACTICAL Help 4
## Ideas of Gifts and Activities for Spiritual Birthdays

### ACTIVITIES

1. Invite friends for a party. If they want to bring a gift, suggest it be something spiritual like a Bible, spiritual book or biography, Scripture plaque, etc. The party provides an opportunity for the host to give his testimony.

2. The parents can also give their child a verse to focus on for the coming year. It is helpful for the very young to have their verse illustrated. One of the first verses our children memorized was "Rejoice always!" The card looked like this:

3. Invite a friend, acquaintance, or missionary over for dinner who has a unique or powerful testimony. Serve the favorite food of the "birthday" child and prompt him or her ahead of time with appropriate questions for the guest.

4. If you are in the Chicago area, you can visit the Billy Graham Museum on the campus of Wheaton College in Wheaton,

Illinois. Explore other museums in your area. You might check local Christian colleges or other organizations to see how they have honored their founders or other significant people.

5. Make this a "giving" birthday instead of a "getting" birthday. Instead of receiving gifts, have the child give something of themselves to someone in need: a song, a picture, a card, a gift, cookies, or bread they have made, etc.

6. Think of a service project that particularly interests your child. Some ideas are:

   a. Collect canned goods and imperishable items from family, friends, or neighbors to give to a soup kitchen.

   b. Put together kits for the homeless in your city and include a toothbrush, toothpaste, deodorant, lotion, tissues, bottle of water, warm socks, and gloves.

   c. One family friend with older children invited guys and girls to a "sweatshirt factory" day. The guys cut out the pattern from the cloth and the girls sewed the shirts. They were sent with another friend who was heading to Romania on a mission trip. What a special memory!

   d. Near his spiritual birthday, when our youngest son was eight years old, we joined Moody Bible Institute students in serving breakfast to the homeless. We went around gently speaking to them loudly enough so they could hear our voice under their covers, but being careful not to touch them, telling them that a hot breakfast was being served around the corner. David will never forget that experience, and it awakened his heart to the needs of others he had not known before.

7. On Michael's first spiritual birthday (he was four years old), we invited my father, his grandfather who shared the same spiritual birthday as he did, to share his testimony of coming to Christ. Grandfather sat on the couch with Michael and his older brother, Will, on either side while I videotaped his conversion story. That recording has become a treasured keepsake and one that we played at my father's memorial service.

8. Have them memorize key Scripture verses dealing with salvation and/or an easily understandable method of explaining salvation.

9. Encourage them to have a yearlong prayer request—perhaps for a family who does not know the Lord yet. Share the prayer burden with them. You will be teaching young ones to pray out loud with someone else. The joy of answered prayer is that much sweeter.

## GIFTS

1. *Dangerous Journey* by Olivere Hunkin—a children's book based on John Bunyan's *Pilgrim's Progress*. Our sons loved this book! It is beautifully illustrated and beautifully depicts Christian principles and experiences.

2. Lead them in learning to explain The Wordless Book. Teach them the song that goes with the book. There is also a salvation story cube that "unfolds" as the story progresses that fascinates young and old. It can be obtained through *E3 Resources* (http://store.e3resources.org).

3. One of my favorite videos is *EE-Taow* produced by New Tribes Mission. It wonderfully portrays the teaching process and eventual conversion of a whole tribe of primitive people. Children and adults are captivated. It is an effective tool in showing the great power of the gospel to transform lives. An effective book in teaching the very young the story line of the Bible is *The Big Picture Story Bible* by David Helm, published by Crossway Books.

4. Other favorite edifying videos are:
   a. *Sheffey* produced by Bob Jones University—based on a true story of a nineteenth-century circuit preacher.

   b. *When Things Seem Impossible* produced by New Tribes Mission. The testimony of a missionary's escape from guerrillas in the jungle of Colombia.

   c. *The Printing* produced by Bob Jones University—based on a true story of Russian Christians printing and distributing the Bible during the Cold War.

d. *The End of the Spear* produced by Every Tribe Entertainment—based on Steve Saint's autobiography.

e. *Flywheel* produced by the Sherwood Baptist Church in Albany, Georgia. It follows the life of a used car salesman before and after his conversion and skillfully incorporates many godly principles.

f. *The Taliabo Story* produced by New Tribes Mission. A story of a primitive Asian tribe looking expectantly for someone to come and share with them the story of deliverance, and what happened when missionaries finally came to live with them, learn their language, and share the gospel.

Chapter
Five

# Hosting a
# *"Blessing"*
# *Party*

What could inspire a young boy to influence the lives of millions of people in many countries of the world?

Before Gipsy Smith had ever taken one of his forty plus evangelistic trips and before he had even become a Christian, D. L. Moody and Ira Sankey visited a gypsy encampment outside of London, England. (The gypsies had not been allowed to attend their crusade meetings in London for fear of their pick-pocketing the large crowds that came to hear Moody preach.) Following the London crusade, Moody and Sankey held a meeting with the group. Afterward, as they prepared to get into their buggy and ride back to London, Ira Sankey, who was Moody's song leader, called back to one of the young men, "The Lord make a preacher of you, my boy."

Ira Sankey probably had no idea that these few simple words would pierce the heart of Rodney "Gipsy" Smith in such a profound way. At that time Rodney had never attended a day of school in his life, but the verbal blessing of Ira Sankey empowered him to a life of great eternal significance.

## THE POWER OF BLESSING

A concerned father in the midst of seeking to consciously shepherd his two daughters was unconscious of the power of his words. He was so proud of the spiritual interests of one of his daughters and would tell her, "You're going to be our missionary and God is going to do great things through you." This godly vision enabled her to resist the pull of the world, follow the Lord, and become a missionary. Her older sister experienced pressure to conform to the world and developed wrong friendships. Out of fear and great concern her father would say, "You are going to become just like your friends." He in effect was not blessing his daughter but giving her a vision for failure that she later fulfilled.

We need to make it perfectly clear that God is the source of blessing. He is the source of every good and perfect gift (James 1:17). His greatest plan includes His desires to bless all peoples through a descendent of Abraham: "In you all the families of the earth shall be blessed" (Genesis 12:3). This promise was fulfilled in Christ who is the promised descendent of Abraham (Galatians 3:16). When one trusts Jesus Christ as their Savior, they are given every spiritual blessing:

> Blessed be the God and Father of our Lord Jesus Christ, who has blessed us with every spiritual blessing in the heavenly places in Christ. (Ephesians 1:3)

The goal of every believer is to experience the blessings that have been given to us in Christ. Loving and faithful obedience does not earn God's blessings, but it does lead to the experience of them. James tells us that it is the one who obeys God's Word who is blessed in what he or she does (1:25).

God charged Aaron and his sons with the task of speaking blessing to His people (Numbers 6:22–27). Once again it is God who was the source of the blessing, but He used others to speak blessing to His people. In the New Testament every Christian is a priest (1 Peter 2:9), and all of us are charged with speaking blessing to each other. In fact we are even told to bless those who curse us (Luke 6:28).

## AN EVENT OF BLESSING

The focus of this chapter is on hosting a blessing party for a loved one. My wife and I have been entrusted with three sons and have had an event on each of their thirteenth birthdays, something like a Christian version of a Bar Mitzvah. The application of this occasion could certainly be broader, and you could do it for a daughter, a spouse, a parent, or any relative or friend.

The mechanics of hosting this event are not complicated. You can write a simple letter to those who you wish to invite and explain the purpose of the occasion (see Practical Help 5 on page 56 for a sample). I opened the program by thanking God for my son and for each of the fathers and sons who were present. I sought to give a verbal blessing to each boy attending the occasion with his father. The blessing highlighted some quality that I saw God working in the boy's life. A few examples are:

"Brad, you have great creative strength and gifting and are not vulnerable to peer pressure."

"Brendan, you have great intellectual and spiritual aptitude and are developing into a person who can stand alone for the Lord."

"Jeremy, you have a great sense of determination and drive as well as a strong sense of justice."

At this point each father and man (some were single) spoke their blessing and advice to my son who had just turned thirteen. They had also written out their remarks and submitted it to us which we put into a scrapbook to provide a permanent written record of the occasion (see Practical Help 6, page 57). Each father concluded their time of sharing with a prayer for my son and all the boys.

*The goal of every believer is to experience the blessings that have been given to us in Christ.*

Thirteen challenges were presented next. As my wife gathered the thirteen balloons, my son Will played the piano and we worshiped God together in song. Will then popped the thirteen balloons, each of which contained a challenge. All of the challenges were read aloud as well as the potential reward for fulfilling them (see Practical Help 7a and 7b, pages 58–59 for the list of challenges). After the challenges the men and boys fellowshipped and had some light refreshments.

## WHEN THE BLESSING IS MISSING

This is great potential as a simple gathering coming together in the name of the Lord to bless each other. It is so easy to "curse" our children. Do you realize that 90 percent of people in jail were told they would be there? They were given a vision for failure. Let God work in your heart to realize the great potential we each have to curse, rather than bless, others.

God's grace can heal the hurts of our hearts and deliver us from bitterness and even overcome the "curses" we ourselves may have been given in the past. If you have been hurt, belittled, accused, and told that you are not of any value, do not continue to pass on this view to others. Seek God in the authority of Christ, and let Him heal your heart at the deepest level and deliver you from bondages to feelings of rejections, failures, jealousy, and shame. Choose God's forgiveness, and seek to bless those who have cursed you. There is no other pathway to freedom. Apart from the grace of God our mouths will be filled with curses and bitterness (see Romans 3:14)!

*This blessing is not to be confined to a single celebration.*

This blessing is not to be confined to a single celebration. God desires it to be a lifestyle that reflects His kind heart to bless. Seek to discern the needs in others, and ask God for opportunities to bless them with God's hopeful truth. In Practical Help 8 on page 60, I have listed some common needs and appropriate scriptural blessings. Even as you discipline a child you can bless him by telling him of your love for him and how you believe God has a special plan for him. Such blessing makes one sense God's value of them and gives them hope for the future. The effect of the blessing is in the sovereign hand of God. This world could use more people like "Gipsy" Smith and Ira Sankey, who spoke blessing to him.

The power of a blessing may go further than you ever dreamed, and it certainly doesn't need to be limited to a thirteenth birthday. It can be at any landmark time of life. You can also select special birthdays to host a blessing party—such as a 21st, 40th, 50th, or 60th birthday. For my 50th, my wife asked me if I desired a big celebration. I told her that I did not, but I would like a series of intimate prayer meetings. On these occasions, some kind friends prayed over me asking God to give me wisdom in using the remainder of my days. I will always cherish these prayers.

## PENNY'S Thoughts

When Will was twelve he asked for thirteen challenges after reading about a missionary kid in Africa who wanted to be challenged in areas of his strengths and weaknesses. Bill and I liked the idea too, and we were thrilled that Will wanted to be stretched! Michael followed in Will's steps, and the result is two different lists of challenges that we prayerfully arrived at after considering their spiritual, intellectual, social, and physical strengths and weaknesses.

Our sons felt an incredible sense of accomplishment after completing the thirteen challenges. Their smiles were absolutely priceless as they got in the car with Bill and their favorite snack foods heading south to their first live Auburn football game. I included a note telling how proud I was of them. I tried to photograph each of their milestones as they checked off the challenges one by one which I compiled in a memory album. It begins with the invitation to the blessing party, photos of each father and son who attended, and exhortation these wonderful friends wrote.

You can, of course, use the idea of blessing for daughters (it was from a family with girls that we got this idea in the first place). And you'll want to use challenges that are unique to your own family. We have found that thirteen is a good age for a blessing party and challenges, but you might prefer to do this at a landmark event or pivotal time, such as a graduation, end of a school year, sixteenth birthday. God will honor your effort as you trust Him.

# PRACTICAL Help 5
## Invitation Letter

14 January 2003
Dear Kent,

On February 2 from 2:00 to 4:30, we would like to have a surprise event to celebrate Will's entrance into a new phase of life as he has turned thirteen. It will be a simple gathering of men and boys, and your presence will mean so much. There will be a time that each person will have a brief opportunity to share a word of encouragement to Will noting some character quality that the Lord is building in him. You may also include a challenge or any piece of advice that has helped you in being a man of God. If you would kindly type your challenge or counsel out, we will compile a little notebook to commemorate this event.

We will conclude the time with prayers offered for God's continuing work in Will. Thank you for your valued investment in the life of our family. Kindly RSVP to Penny or me and try to keep it a surprise.

In Christ's love,
Bill Thrasher

# PRACTICAL Help 6
## Blessing Letter

28 January 2003
Dear Will,

You are truly a gift of God to our family. Prior to your birth, God impressed upon my spirit Luke 1:14, which also anticipates the birth of a son: "You will have joy and gladness and many will rejoice at his birth." Like John the Baptist who pointed people to Jesus, I sensed that your life would be a joy to God, a joy to us, and a joy to others. In Scripture the key to joy is righteousness (Hebrews 1:9), and I have been so comforted by this promise. You have truly been a source of joy to me during these thirteen years!

When you were born with some extra capillaries, blood vessels, and lymphs on your left arm and hand, God gave me special comfort from Matthew 1. The message of comfort was from the principle I derived from Matthew 1:20–21. The comfort was to in no way fear, but that many would benefit from his life.

You have a very tender heart to the Lord and others. You have always been so quick to ask forgiveness. I can remember times that you have gotten out of bed to come to our room and ask forgiveness for a small matter in order to keep a clear con- science before the Lord.

You are a precious son. Satan lusts to destroy you, but rest in Romans 8:31, "If God is for us, who is against us?" I prayed from your birth that our hearts would always be knit together, and I believe God has and is answering that prayer.

Always remember that in God you have a perfect Father. Let Him love you and bless you with the certainty that you belong to Him and He will never leave you or forsake you (Isaiah 44:3–5; Hebrews 13:5).

With all our love,
Mom and Dad

# PRACTICAL Help 7a
## First Example of Thirteen Challenges

I. Complete your memory goal of 225 verses.
2. Run thirty miles in thirty days.
3. Produce our spring family newsletter on the computer.
4. Memorize all Greek vocabulary words used over 200 times in the New Testament.
5. Conquer one of the bar chords on the guitar.
6. Teach part of a family class Sunday school.
7. Interview three men in different professions that interest you and write any insight you have about God's plan for your life.
8. In the summer, do a biographical Bible study on the life of Daniel.
9. Read three classic books assigned by Mom and Dad.
IO. Cook a meal for the family.
II. Run a IOk race.
I2. Write up your testimony for baptism.
I3. Write out your conviction about courtship.

## REWARD

Your choice:   I. Two White Sox baseball games
               2. Attend an Auburn football game with Dad.

# PRACTICAL Help 7b
## Second Example of Thirteen Challenges

1. Read three of Daddy's books and finish reading through the Bible.
2. Memorize Matthew 5–7 and the book of Philippians.
3. Learn Bible study methods from an Old Testament narrative, Psalms, a Gospel, and an epistle.
4. Every week for fifteen weeks write notes of gratefulness to men in leadership or people who need encouragement.
5. Plan a social event at our home by inviting the guests, preparing the food, and planning the evening.
6. Master typing, PowerPoint, and Excel.
7. Interview three men in different professions interesting to you, and write any insight you have about God's plan for your life.
8. Be involved in various community services: CareNet Pregnancy Center, Twice As Nice, homeless shelter, Kids Club, and church nursery or any other church needs.
9. Learn new housing or fatherly skills.
10. Run thirty miles in thirty days and develop push-up and sit-up goals.
11. Learn Latin and Greek roots.
12. Ask God for three ways to bless your brothers. Plan with Mom and Dad.
13. Develop courtship convictions.

## REWARD

Your choice:  1. Two White Sox baseball games
2. Attend an Auburn football game with Dad.

## PRACTICAL Help 8

**Blessings That Meet Needs**

| NEED | BLESSING | |
|---|---|---|
| Fear | Courage | Psa. 34:4; I John 4:18 |
| Anxiety | Peace | I Pet. 5:7 |
| Temptation | Delight in God | Psa. 37:4 |
| | Trust in God | Prov. 3:1–6 |
| Lack of Vision | Success | John 17:4 |
| Feel Inadequate | Adequacies in God | 2 Cor. 3:5 |
| Feel Unloved | Love | John 17:23 |
| Despair | Hope | Rom. 15:13 |
| Anger | Love and Forgiveness | I Pet. 3:9 |
| Ungodly Lust | Purity | I Thess. 4:3–5 |

Simply pray that in Jesus' name that God would bless with courage, peace, a delight and trust in God, godly success, a knowledge of Christ's adequacies, love, hope, forgiveness, and purity. You can expand this list as you mine the treasures of the riches we have in Christ.

# Section Three
## *Good Friday and Easter*

Chapter
Six

Entering
into the
*Meaning of
Good Friday*

When you take a vacation, do you have a particular objective for it?

Maybe your goal is to simply experience a change of pace and refresh your body. I knew of one intense pastor who took one month off a year just to build himself back up physically. When our physical batteries are restored, we also need to pay attention to our spiritual life. For example, Lewis Sperry Chafer, the founder of Dallas Seminary, took a study vacation with the goal of reading through the New Testament and noting everything that happens to a person when they become a Christian. He noted thirty-three things!

Every blessing of God flows to us through the cross. Romans 1:18–3:20 clearly presents mankind's desperate lot of being under God's wrath with no human hope. At this point the Romans commentator Stifler tells us that God is introduced into the action because the plot has gotten into such a tangle that only He can unravel it[1] (see Romans 3:21–26). Good Friday is an opportunity to remember the glorious accomplishments of the cross.

After breakfast, I gathered my family around the breakfast table and, on a white board, wrote the word "redemption." I then proceeded to explain it. I will give you each of the words I wrote and the brief explanation that I gave.

## REDEMPTION

The Bible portrays man as enslaved to sin or his own self-will (Romans 6:18), the curse of the Law (Galatians 3:13), Satan (Colossians 1:13), and death (Hebrews 2:15). The result is a life that is called vain, futile, or empty (1 Peter 1:18). There is only one key that is able to unlock our prison door. Without it we are doomed to this empty way of life and to share our life with one whose heart is full of deceit and destruction (John 8:44). The key is the precious blood of Jesus Christ (1 Peter 1:19). Christ's death on the cross delivers us from slavery to sin to being a slave of righteousness (Romans 6:18), from the condemnation of the law to under God's gracious favor (Romans 6:14), from Satan's dominion to the rule of Christ (Colossians 1:13), and from the slavery of death to the experience of eternal life (John 17:3). The futile life (1 Peter 1:18) is replaced with a life Jesus called abundant (John 10:10).

*Good Friday is an opportunity to remember the glorious accomplishments of the cross.*

We can celebrate Good Friday in declaring that the totality of our lives belongs to our wonderful God and that the devil has no right to any facet of our life. We have been redeemed by His precious blood and even have the hope of one day receiving a new, glorious, redeemed body (Romans 8:23).

| WHAT CHRIST'S REDEEMING BLOOD HAS ACCOMPLISHED | |
|---|---|
| Past Bondage | Present Freedom |
| Slavery to Sin (Romans 6:18) | Slavery to Righteousness (Romans 6:18) |
| Condemnation of the Law (Galatians 3:13) | God's Gracious Favor (Romans 6:14) |
| Satan's Dominion (Colossians 1:13) | The Rule of Christ (Colossians 1:13) |
| Slavery of Death (Hebrews 2:15) | Experience of Eternal Life (John 17:3) |
| Vain and Empty Life (I Peter 1:18) | Abundant Life (John 10:10) |

## PROPITIATION

One word is not enough to capture the multifaceted accomplishment of the cross. Propitiation is the God-ward side of Jesus' death. His righteousness demands that sin must be punished by His wrath. His wrath abides on all who resist His kind provision for salvation (John 3:36). However, Jesus' death frees the believer from God's condemning wrath because God's righteousness is completely satisfied with Christ's death. You do not have to "make God willing" to forgive you. He is faithful and righteous to cleanse you from all unrighteousness as you confess your sins to Him as His child (1 John 1:9).

| WHAT CHRIST'S PROPITIATION MEANS TO A BELIEVER | |
| --- | --- |
| **Past** | **Present** |
| Under God's condemning wrath | Object of God's kindness and the knowledge that God's righteousness has been fully satisfied with Christ's payment for my sin |

## RECONCILIATION

As we celebrate Good Friday, it is important to note from *what* we have been rescued. We were formerly alienated from God as the barrier of our sin estranged us from God. Jesus' death and resurrection removed this barrier and enables the believer to enjoy peace with God (Romans 5:1, 10; cf. 2 Corinthians 5:18–20)!

| WHAT CHRIST'S RECONCILIATION MEANS TO A BELIEVER | |
| --- | --- |
| **Past** | **Present** |
| Alienated from God and an Enemy of God | Permanent Peace with God |

## DELIVERANCE FROM SIN'S POWER

All of mankind is not only under the guilt of sin, but also under the control of sin. God's plan of salvation provides a remedy for both! Jesus died to set the believer free from being enslaved to his own self-will. Sin can now be resisted and every facet of our beings can be presented to the Lord as instruments of righteousness (Romans 6:12–13). On Good Friday, let the Spirit of God speak hope to your spirit in regard to your greatest struggle. His death released you to be able to struggle victoriously as you experience the joy of committing your battles to the Lord.

| Past | Present |
|------|---------|
| Controlled by Sin— A Self-willed Life | Freed to Live as I Was Created to Live and Enjoy God |

## DEFEAT OF SATAN

The Bible tells us that our ultimate enemy is the devil and his well-organized army of demonic spirits (Ephesians 6:11–12). The believer is not to be ignorant of Satan's schemes (2 Corinthians 2:11). He seeks to deceive us and promote doubt and rebellion to God and His ways. Jesus' death righteously paid for our sin and released us from Satan's kingdom to live under His righteous rule (Colossians 1:13).

| Past | Present |
|------|---------|
| Under Satan's Cruel Dominion | Live in Victory over Satan's Destructive Lies and Power |

## PROVISION FOR CLEANSING

The Bible speaks of forgiveness in two ways. First, it speaks of His judicial forgiveness. This is the forgiveness that one experiences the moment they trust Christ. It enables all of their sins to be wiped clean that they might be brought into a relationship with a holy God. It is this forgiveness that the apostle John is speaking of in 1 John 2:12, "I am writing to you, little children, because your sins have been forgiven you." To the same people who have been forgiven, he instructs them to "walk in the Light" and confess their sins in order to be forgiven and cleansed (1 John 1:7, 9). Secondly, these later verses speak of what I am terming "family forgiveness." Jesus' death that you celebrate on Good Friday provides for not only the forgiveness that brings you into a relationship with God, but also the forgiveness that enables you to walk in fellowship with a holy God!

| Past | Present |
|------|---------|
| Guilt and an Unclean Conscience | Continually Enjoying Cleansing Forgiveness and a Life under an "Unclouded Heaven" |

## BASIS FOR NEW COVENANT

Jesus instructed a new covenant through the blood sacrifice of His death. The Passover that He celebrated with His disciples prior to His death anticipated this sacrifice, and the ordinances of the Lord's Table now commemorate it (cf. Matthew 26:28).

It is important for every child of God to see himself or herself in a covenant relationship with God. The Lord has solemnly pledged to do certain things for us. When people get married, they make vows that hold them accountable to fulfill very solemn obligations. When I speak at weddings I have reminded the bride and groom of Christ's vows to them as a support and encouragement to fulfill their vows to each other.

The new covenant was originally given to Israel, but it is clear that the church shares in this new covenant (cf. 2 Corinthians 3). In this new covenant God has pledged to forgive us:

> Then I will sprinkle clean water on you, and you will be clean; I will cleanse you from all your filthiness and from all your idols. (Ezekiel 36:25)

Stare at this verse and worship God for His glorious forgiveness. He has also pledged to enable us:

> I will put My Spirit within you and cause you to walk in My statutes, and you will be careful to observe My ordinances. (Ezekiel 36:27)

Praise Him for His enablement as you humble yourself before Him and contemplate your greatest challenges. Good Friday is a glorious reminder to rejoice in His covenant promises to you!

| Past | Present |
|------|---------|
| Alienated from God | In a Glorious Covenant Relationship with God Who Has Promised to Forgive and Enable |

## SUBSTITUTION

Christ redeemed us from the curse of the Law, having become a curse for us—for it is written, "Cursed is everyone who hangs on a tree." (Galatians 3:13)

Jesus Christ is our substitution who died for our sins, and as Peter puts it "the just for the unjust" (1 Peter 3:18). When you trust Christ as your substitute, do you realize how wonderful it is?

He bore our curse that He might give us His blessings. I compiled the following list you can use as a starting point in praising God for His blessings that are yours.

| CURSES | BLESSINGS |
|---|---|
| Condemnation | Boldness |
| Bondage | Acceptance and Love |
| Oppression | Freedom of God's Control |
|  | Light Load and Freedom |
| Impurity | Purity |
| Prejudice | Love |
| Legalism | Liberty |
| Humiliation | Exaltation |
| Barrenness | Fruitfulness |
| Hopelessness | Hope |
| Lies | Truth |
| Idolatry | True Worship |
| Fear | Confidence and Love |
| Lack of Provision, Direction | Provision and Direction |
| Dishonor | Glorify God |
| Forsaken | Never Left or Abandoned |

Are you living in light of these blessings? On the authority of Christ's shed blood, believe God to deliver you from these curses and lead you into the full experiences of these blessings.

## GLORIFY GOD'S CHARACTER

The final accomplishment of the cross is the glorification of God's name. Jesus prayed in anticipation of His death, "Father glorify your name." The Father responded with the words, "I have both glorified it, and will glorify it again" (John 12:28). God's name speaks of His revealed character and attributes. When Jesus died He displayed God's love, mercy, and grace. The cross also displayed His holiness and righteousness in requiring a payment for sin in order to righteously forgive. It displayed God's wisdom in devising a plan where He could be righteous and gracious at the same time. It showed His faithfulness to His sovereign plan of redemption which He had planned before the world began. Truly the cross glorifies God's character.

These are some of the ways to worship our wonderful God as you celebrate Good Friday. You can make the length and details of your explanation appropriate to the age and spiritual maturity of the ones you are addressing. You may want to limit the scope of your celebration to only one of the Lord's accomplishments on the cross. You can then look up appropriate Bible verses that focus on this particular work of the cross.

*When Jesus died He displayed God's love, mercy, and grace.*

If your children are too young to read, you can illustrate one of the concepts. Perhaps you have heard of the man with the empty birdcage.

When walking along one day, he noticed a boy carrying a cage filled with birds. The birds didn't seem to be well cared for, nor were they singing. The man asked the boy, "What are you going to do with those birds?"

"I am going to keep them in this cage forever."

"I'll buy them from you," the kind man offered. "I will give you ten dollars."

"Oh, sure, I'll sell them!" the boy replied.

The man purchased the birds and then set them free. They flew away singing joyfully. This is a picture of redemption—Christ purchased us from a cruel master and set us free. The Spirit of God can relate this truth even to a very young mind.

Spend time in prayer thanking Christ for His wonderful work that you celebrate on Good Friday. Consider attending a Good Friday service at your church. And most of all, enjoy your celebration.

## PENNY'S Thoughts

Oh, how I love this holiday! As a mom, I would encourage all you mothers to let these spiritual truths that Bill outlined rest deeply in your souls. Take time in the week or two weeks before Easter to meditate on them and praise God for His incredible provisions for us. Your spirit so affects the children, and they will "catch" your excitement, gratefulness, and worshipful spirit.

One Easter one of my sons emerged from our workroom with three crosses he had made from lumber and nails. He was interacting with the Passion Week. It might have been a response to Robert Doares's book *Immanuel: God with Us: The Life of Christ in Art* (Crossway), which I loved to use with my young children. This book is a series of historically accurate scenes from Jesus' life that Doares drew for his devotions. As I read from the Bible, they feast their eyes on this beautiful artwork.

### OTHER IDEAS:

1. Display a cross with crown of thorns on the mantel or in a prominent place in your home. (Remove it early Easter morning.) Ask the children, *Why did Jesus have to die on the cross?*

2. If you have a model of the tomb keep the stone over the entrance. Have the children roll the stone away Easter morning.

3. Act out aspects of the Good Friday story;
   a. Role-play what it was like for the disciples—women included—to see Jesus on the cross.
   b. Act out the apostles trying to stay awake to pray and falling asleep.

    c. What was it like in the garden when the apostles saw Him arrested?

4. Think about Peter—why did he deny knowing Jesus? Do we ever pretend we don't know about Jesus? Are we ever embarrassed or afraid to talk about Him?
5. You may want to consider making this a day of fasting. For ideas, see *Journey to Victorious Praying*, pages 140–60.

NOTE

1. James Stifler, *The Epistle to the Romans* (Chicago: Moody, 1983), 58–66.

_Chapter Seven_

Living in the
Light of the
_Meaning
of Easter_

Many years ago I read an article about the uniqueness of Jesus Christ. It was one of the things God used to solidify a surrender of my life to Him and to later discern His call to teach and preach His Word. Christ claimed to be the unique Son of God, and even His enemies clearly understood that He was claiming full equality with God (cf. John 5:18). It was His resurrection that declared to the world that His claim is true (Romans 1:4)!

## PREEMINENT ABOVE ALL OTHERS

There is no better way to celebrate Easter than to take time to fall at His feet and to declare Him to be your Lord and your God (cf. John 20:28). One day everyone will acknowledge Him (Philippians 2:9–11), but we can now freely live in light of the truth that we worship a living Savior. Take time on this day to declare His absolute uniqueness from every other religious leader or person. Search your own heart to see if He is truly preeminent above all others in your devotion and affections.

## TRUE TO ALL HIS PROMISES

The resurrection of Christ calls for a special celebration. This miraculous event not only vindicated Jesus as the unique Son of God but also showed His words and promises to be true. The angel's declaration to His desperate followers who had come to the grave was, "Do not be afraid; for I know that you are looking for Jesus who has been crucified. He is not here, for He has risen, just as He said. Come, see the place where He was lying" (Matthew 28:5–6).

As we humble ourselves before Him and experience His gracious promises, we honor our resurrected Lord. You may invite a certain guest to your Easter celebration to be prepared to share a promise on which they are standing.

## THE PROMISE OF PARDON

Christ promised to have the authority to forgive sin. His word to the paralytic, "Son, your sins are forgiven" (Mark 2:5), was substantiated by His miraculous healing of the man. Those who trust Christ experience His pardon and are declared righteous because He imputes Christ's perfect obedience to our account. He "was raised because of our justification" are the words of Romans 4:25. On Easter, take time to thank Him and praise Him for His complete and gracious pardon.

> When you were dead in your transgressions and the uncircumcision of your flesh, He made you alive together with Him, having forgiven us all our transgressions, having canceled out the certificate of debt consisting of decrees against us, which was hostile to us; and He has taken it out of the way, having nailed it to the cross. (Colossians 2:13–14)

You may let someone at your Easter dinner celebration share their testimony about how they have experienced Christ's forgiveness. We have chosen to give special attention to a guest at times by serving their meal on a special plate that says "You Are Loved" around its rim. If this special guest knows the Lord, give them an opportunity to share their testimony. Take time this Easter to praise God for His promises.

## THE PROMISE OF PURPOSE

People realize their purpose when they realize who they are— a creation by God the Son—and when they realize why they are here on this earth—to live for God the Son. We are created by Him and *"for Him"* (Colossians 1:16). Christ died and rose again to free us from only living for ourselves:

> For the love of Christ controls us, having concluded this, that one died for all, therefore all died; and He died for all, so that they who live might no longer live for themselves, but for Him who died and rose again on their behalf. (2 Corinthians 5:14–15)

Our life on this earth needs the perspective of eternity in order for it to make sense:

> For I consider that the sufferings of this present time are not worthy to be compared with the glory that is to be revealed to us. (Romans 8:18)

Christ's resurrection was a literal bodily resurrection. It is the hope of our bodily resurrection that drives away the fear of death and gives us the perspective and assurance of an eternal purpose. We can confidently know that the One who raised Jesus from the dead will also raise us (2 Corinthians 4:14)! We are to replace the fear of man, who at most can kill the body, with the fear of God as we live for Him (Matthew 10:28). The prospect of the Lord's coming and our being given a new redeemed body is a vital part of the celebration of Easter (Romans 8:23).

*Take time this Easter to praise God for His promises.*

## THE PROMISE OF POWER

The apostle Paul longed to know Christ and the power of His resurrection (Philippians 3:10). What he longed to experience himself, he also prayed for other believers to likewise joyfully experience (Ephesians 1:18–20).

What does it mean to experience resurrection power? It means to experience victory over our own self-will (flesh), and the ability to live a new life (Romans 6:4). Resurrection power is also the power that gives victory out of apparent defeat. When Christ was in the grave, matters looked hopeless for it appeared that the enemies of unrighteousness had triumphed. However, in that very moment of apparent defeat, God was winning a great victory and then came the resurrection! Some excellent resources are the books *They Found the Secret*,[1] *Seventy Years of Miracles*,[2] and *Courageous Christians*.[3] These books contain short accounts of people who discovered the open secret of experiencing God's power in their lives. They make for great personal or family reading.

What does it mean to experience resurrection power? In which circumstances in your life do you need to trust God for His resurrection power? What a glorious way to celebrate Easter as not only a historical fact but also a daily reality! You might take time to rehearse past experience with your loved ones at how God turned a great disappointment and dark time into a special blessing and victory. Edward Kimball was a Sunday school teacher who visited the store where one of his pupils worked. Kimball was quite nervous, but asked the young man to trust Christ. He left the store feeling like a failure at his evangelistic effort; however, his young pupil, D. L. Moody, left the store as a new man and eventually became a prominent evangelist.[4]

Likewise, you and I often might feel like we have not been effective in our service for Christ. However, we too can experience resurrection power. Think what "small thing" Edward Kimball did, and how greatly God multiplied his efforts.

*What does it mean to experience resurrection power?*

Who knows what He can do through you and me? What if you invited a classmate to Sunday school or to youth group and he or she eventually accepted Christ? A whole future generation could have changed lives because of that "small thing." Nothing is beyond the reach of God's long and loving arm.

Since Christ is a risen Savior (Ephesians 1:20–23) nothing can defeat Him. He is the Lord of everything, and He is the head of the church. He is available to guide and aid His people. He is also able to sympathize with all our weaknesses because He has been tempted in all things (Hebrews 4:15). Celebrate Easter by coming to Him and telling Him about your greatest struggle. As you do, He promises to extend to you mercy—sympathetic understanding and aid—as well as grace—the motivation and enablement that you need to be victorious (Hebrews 4:16).

## THE PROMISE OF PEACE

The Lord's followers were quite perplexed when He announced His imminent death and departure from them. He gave them the promise of peace.

Peace I leave with you; My peace I give to you; not as the world gives do I give to you. Do not let your heart be troubled, nor let it be fearful. (John 14:27)

It was my desire for true peace that drew me to a surrender to Christ. This peace involves, first and foremost, peace with God. This flows out of the truth of one's justification.

Therefore, having been justified by faith, we have peace with God through our Lord Jesus Christ. (Romans 5:1)

This peace is also a peace with other believers.

For He Himself is our peace, who made both groups into one and broke down the barrier of the dividing wall. (Ephesians 2:14)

It is Christ's death and resurrection that secured this peace. We are to strive in God's strength to maintain the unity that He has established (Ephesians 4:3) and as far as it depends on us to be at peace with all people (Romans 12:18). Perhaps seeking reconciliation with someone needs to be a part of your celebration of Easter!

The peace is also a peace with oneself that comes from casting all our cares upon Him and unburdening our hearts. What anxiety do you need to talk to the Lord about this Easter?

Be anxious for nothing, but in everything by prayer and supplication with thanksgiving let your requests be made known to God. And the peace of God, which surpasses all comprehension, will guard your hearts and your minds in Christ Jesus. (Philippians 4:6–7)

Easter is a special holiday. We are to be reminded of it every Lord 's day as well as every day of our lives as we worship Him and rest in His promises of *pardon, purpose, power,* and *peace.* Let Easter be a special holiday in which you seek to share and experience these wonderful spiritual truths in the midst of your celebration.

# PRACTICAL Help 9
## Ideas for Easter Celebration

- Awaken your children with the joyous phrase "He is risen!" Teach them the response, "He is risen indeed!" Ask them why the resurrection was so important. (It signifies that God accepted Jesus' payment for our sins with His blood, and Jesus has conquered sin and death!)
- Resurrection Eggs—plastic eggs that you can purchase with resurrection symbols inside.
- Read *My First Story of Easter* by Tim Dowley.
- Make Resurrection Buns

     Flatten a Grand (or other large) canned biscuit until it is about five inches across. Melt butter and spread the butter, as well as cinnamon and sugar, on the dough. The spices are symbolic of the anointing of Jesus' body before His burial.

Place a large marshmallow in the center of the dough, explaining that it stands for Jesus—the white represents His pure and sinless life. Then fold the sides around the marshmallow forming a "tomb." (Be sure to pinch the sides down firmly so they do not open while baking.) Coat the outside with more melted butter, cinnamon, and sugar.

Bake following the package directions. Allow the buns to cool because the marshmallow will be very hot.

When you bite into the buns, you will discover that they are empty—the marshmallow has melted.

- Have children make an empty tomb out of Legos to put on the Easter cake.

- Around this time of year we celebrate the coming of spring and "resurrection of life." It is special to remind our children of God's faithfulness—that there will always be springtime and harvest, as long as the sun and moon endure. We pay special attention to the returning of the robin, which is a sign of spring. Whoever spots the first robin gets to choose a restaurant to celebrate the beginning of this fun season.

- Play the latter part of Handel's *Messiah*, helping the children understand the words.

- Have a hymn-sing, inviting other families to join you in singing resurrection hymns and spiritual songs.

- Memorize portions or all of I Corinthians 15.

- Discuss how the resurrection makes Christianity different from all other religions.

- Find out how the date for Easter is determined. Why is it different each year? What is the difference in the way the orthodox and western churches choose the date?

- Display on the Easter dining room table various larger place cards on beautiful papers praising God with phrases like:

> Behold the Lamb of God!
> Hallelujah! What a Savior!
> King of Kings

> Lord of Lords
> Prince of Peace
> Wonderful Counselor
> He shall reign forever!

- Make a banner for your front door saying, "Hallelujah! What a Savior!"

- One Easter, at a larger celebration, we asked the following questions to stimulate spiritual conversation. The table that gets the most points gets served the dessert first. They can determine which point question they desire, and if they answer it they get the points.

1. 10 Points: What verse of Scripture do you feel strongly about because you KNOW that it is true since you have experienced it in a profound way? Why?
2. 5 Points: If you could read only one section of the newspaper, what section would it be? Why?
3. 15 Points: God says, that all things "work together for good." Is there something "bad" or uncomfortable that has happened to you that you can now see as a "good" thing?
4. 5 Points: In what way are you like one of your parents?
5. 10 Points: What advice did one of your parents give you for which you are thankful? Why?
6. 5 Points: What is a question that people should ask you? (What do you like to talk about?)
7. 10 Points: Who is a teacher for which you are especially thankful and why?
8. 5 Points: What is a fond memory of yours and why?
9. 10 Points: What is something that has happened during the last year for which you are thankful and why?
10. 5 Points: What is one of your favorite hobbies and why?
11. 10 Points: What book, other than the Bible, has changed your life and how?
12. 5 Points: Select one of your elementary teachers. How would they have described you when they were your teacher? Why?

NOTES

1. V. Raymond Edman, *They Found the Secret* (Grand Rapids: Zondervan, 1984).
2. Richard Harvey, *Seventy Years of Miracles* (Camp Hill, PA: Horizon Books, 1992).
3. Joyce Vollmer Brown, *Courageous Christians* (Chicago: Moody, 2000).
4. This principle is further explained in my book *A Journey to Victorious Praying.*

# Section Four
*Thanksgiving*

Chapter
Eight

# Ideas for
# *Celebrating*
# *Thanksgiving*

Thanksgiving is one of my favorite holidays, mostly for the reason that it is potentially one of the purest. It is not as pervaded by the materialistic drives that creep into the other holidays. However, even Thanksgiving can degenerate into becoming only a feast rather than a true day of thanking God for His blessings. One Thanksgiving Eve, Senate Chaplain Peter Marshall prayed, "Let not feasting, football, and festivity end in forgetfulness of God." The last lines of his prayer contained a mild rebuke to those who would neglect to thank Him for all we have and yet ask Him for more!

## THE HOSTS OF THANKSGIVING PAST

Something that is often lacking in our present day is an accurate knowledge of the past. One way to celebrate Thanksgiving is to educate our loved ones about its heritage. Governor William Bradford came to America on the Mayflower with his first wife, Dorothy. (Dorothy drowned in 1620 when she accidentally fell overboard while the ship was anchored in Provincetown Harbor; Bradford remarried in August of 1623.) Despite the many hardships the Pilgrims had endured in their first three years in the new land, the governor declared November 29, 1623, a day for "rendering thanksgiving to ye Almighty God for all His blessings." This official announcement in their third year in the new continent made official what they had already done on their first year when Chief Massasoit and about ninety other native Americans celebrated a three-day thanksgiving feast with the Pilgrims in 1621.

Samuel Adams issued a proclamation on November 1, 1777, that was adopted by the thirteen states declaring December 18 as a day of "solemn Thanksgiving and praise, that with one heart and one voice the good people may express the grateful feelings of their hearts and consecrate themselves to the service of their divine benefactor."

On October 3, 1789, military hero George Washington, who was serving as the first president of the United States of America, declared November 26 as a day of public thanksgiving and prayer. Eighty-four years later with our country at war against itself, Abraham Lincoln issued a Thanksgiving proclamation on October 3, 1863, declaring the fourth Tuesday in November as a national Thanksgiving holiday. In 1939 Franklin D. Roosevelt moved the holiday to the third Thursday of November, and then in 1941 moved it to the fourth Thursday in November where it stands today.

Other presidents have also issued Thanksgiving proclamations, including President William McKinley in 1898, Woodrow Wilson in 1920, and George W. Bush in 2001. You can read Washington's and Lincoln's proclamations on pages 93 and 95. Part of our family's tradition is to read the Lincoln Proclamation each year.

## A WEEK OF THANKFUL DAYS

Trying to do something one day out of the year that is foreign to our lifestyle the rest of the year usually isn't very successful. One way to prepare for the holidays is to precede it with a season of thanksgiving. The remainder of this chapter will attempt to outline a possible way to encourage a thanksgiving emphasis for several days.

The following exercise is an assignment that I have given to hundreds of people. I am indebted to an excerpt I read many years ago in *Spirit of Revival* magazine from Life Action Ministry.[1] With some adaptation for your own situation, you'll find this doable with family members of all ages.

On the **first day** simply note what you learn about thanksgiving from the short book of Colossians. You may choose to simply give the key verses and read them and note their contribution to the topic of thanksgiving. Look at Colossians 1:3, 12; 2:7; 3:15, 17; and 4:2.

On the **second day** make a list of the spiritual and material blessing that you have received from the Lord. Read Ephesians 1:3–14 to begin this day's activity.

On the **third day** try to learn this definition of gratefulness—"learning to recognize and express appreciation for the benefits I have received from God and others." As an application to this definition, make a list of the members of your family and write down one thing about each person for which you are grateful. Take time to thank God for each member of the family into which God has sovereignly placed you. Follow this up by expressing gratitude to the person through a note, a phone call, or in person. Tell them that you especially thanked God for them today and share the specific quality in their life for which you are grateful.

On the **fourth day** expand your list to include people outside your family whom God has used to bless your life—friends, neighbors, pastors, teachers, authors, leaders of Christian ministries, and others. Include your mechanic, hair stylist, and insurance agent. Who else can you think of? After you thank God for each of these, ask yourself, "Have I ever thanked that person for how God has used them in my life?" Put a check mark next to each name to which you have expressed gratitude.

*Make a list of each member of your family and write down one thing about each person for which you are grateful.*

On the **fifth day** take time to express to some of them how God has ministered to you through them.

Begin the **sixth day** by reading 1 Thessalonians 5:18:

In everything give thanks; for this is God's will for you in Christ Jesus.

As you go through the entire day make an attempt to cooperate with the Holy Spirit in consciously giving thanks for *all things*—no matter how small or big! One man who did this was prompted to thank God for his toothbrush and then the toothpaste. As he was thanking God, he realized that he had never thanked God for his teeth!

On the **last day** of your thanksgiving emphasis, focus on thanking God for the circumstances, people, and events that provide special difficulty in your life. Expressing thanks is an act of your will, and the emotions may follow much later. It is also an expression of faith in God's sovereignty and goodness as the "Blessed Controller" who is able to work all things together for good. With this in mind write down the difficult things for which you choose to give God thanks. Dr. Helen Roseveare was a missionary doctor in the Congo who was shamefully abused by some rebel soldiers. She found some relief to her painful struggle in attempting to make sense of this when she sensed God asking her to be willing to give thanks for that which she may not be given the privilege to understand this side of heaven.

This seven-day exercise may not necessarily be seven consecutive days. You may choose to take more than one day for a certain activity. I am indebted to the one who inspired this idea and pray that it benefits you as well. Have a blessed Thanksgiving!

## PENNY'S Thoughts

1. For a few years right before Thanksgiving we sent out our family newsletter "Thrasher Thanksgivings" in which we shared our past year's blessings. The writing of this newsletter helped us to think and thank our wonderful God as we prepared our hearts for Thanksgiving.

2. One of our friends has a ceramic pumpkin with a lid in her kitchen. As God makes her aware of the blessings He sends their way throughout the year, she writes it down and puts it in the pumpkin. On Thanksgiving Day they go through

these notes and give gratitude for the way God has shown His great goodness to them.

3. For over twenty years Bill has kept a Jehovah Jireh Journal for our family. *Jehovah Jireh* means the "God who provides." One Thanksgiving we were greatly blessed to recall how God has marvelously provided for us as Bill read the journal to us.

NOTE

1. Adapted from the November 1992 issue of *Spirit of Revival*, volume 22, number 2, 28–31.

# PRACTICAL Help 10
## George Washington's Thanksgiving Proclamation

"A Day of Public Thanksgiving and Prayer"
George Washington
Thanksgiving Proclamation, 1789

Whereas it is the duty of all nations to acknowledge the providence of Almighty God, to obey His will, to be grateful for His benefits, and humbly to implore His protection and favor; and Whereas both Houses of Congress have, by their joint committee, requested me "to recommend to the people of the United States a day of public thanksgiving and prayer, to be observed by acknowledging with grateful hearts the many and signal favors of Almighty God, especially by affording them an opportunity peaceably to establish a form of government for their safety and happiness:" Now therefore, I do recommend and assign Thursday, the 26th day of November next, to be devoted by the people of these States to the service of that great and glorious Being who is the beneficent author of all the good that was, that is, or that will be; that we may then all unite in rendering unto Him our sincere and humble thanks for His kind care and protection of the people of this country previous to their becoming a nation; for the signal and manifold mercies and the favorable interpositions of His providence in the course and conclusion of the late war; for the great degree of tranquility, union, and plenty which we have since enjoyed; for the peaceable and rational manner in which we have been enabled to establish constitutions of government for our safety and happiness, and particularly the national one now lately instituted for the civil and religious liberty with which we are blessed and the means we have of acquiring and diffusing useful knowledge; and, in general, for all the great and various favors which He has been pleased to confer upon us.

And also that we may then unite in most humbly offering our prayers and supplications to the great Lord and Ruler of Nations and beseech Him to pardon our national and other transgressions—to enable us all, whether in public or private stations, to perform our several and relative duties properly and punctually; to render our National Government a blessing to all the people by constantly being a Government of wise, just, and constitutional laws, discreetly and faithfully executed and obeyed; to protect and guide all sovereigns and nations (especially such as have shown kindness unto us); and to bless them with good governments, peace, and concord; to promote the knowledge and practice of true religion and virtue, and the increase of science among them and us; and, generally to grant unto all mankind such a degree of temporal prosperity as He alone knows to be best.

Given under my hand, at the city of New York, the third day of October, A.D. 1789.

(Signed) G. Washington

# PRACTICAL Help 11
## Words of Abraham Lincoln

The following is an anthology of excerpts from Lincoln's Proclamation Appointing a National Day of Prayer and Fasting, Proclamation Appointing a National Fast Day, and Thanksgiving Proclamation :

It is the duty of nations as well as of men to own their dependence upon the overruling power of God; to confess their sins and transgressions in humble sorrow, yet with assured hope that genuine repentance will lead to mercy and pardon; and to recognize the sublime truth, announced in the Holy Scriptures and proven by all history, that those nations are blessed whose God is the Lord.

We know that by His divine law, nations, like individuals, are subjected to punishments and chastisements in this world. May we not justly fear that the awful calamity of civil war which now desolates the land may be a punishment inflicted upon us for our presumptuous sins, to the needful end of our national reformation as a whole people?

We have been the recipients of the choicest bounties of heaven; we have been preserved these many years in peace and prosperity; we have grown in numbers, wealth, and power as no other nation has ever grown. But we have forgotten God. We have forgotten the gracious hand which preserved us in peace and multiplied and enriched and strengthened us, and we have vainly imagined, in the deceitfulness of our hearts, that all these blessings were produced by some superior wisdom and virtue of our own. Intoxicated with unbroken success, we have become too self-sufficient to feel the necessity of redeeming and preserving grace, too proud to pray to the God that made us.

It has seemed to me fit and proper that they should be solemnly, reverently, and gratefully acknowledged, as with one heart and one voice, by the whole American people. I do therefore invite my fellow-citizens in every part of the United States, and also those who are at sea and those who are sojourning in foreign lands, to set apart and observe the last Thursday of November next as a day of thanksgiving and praise to our beneficent Father who dwelleth in the heavens.

Abraham Lincoln

Chapter
Nine

Unleashing the
*Spiritual
Potential of
Thanksgiving*

G ilbert Beers, a prolific author, tells the story of his great-great-grandmother—to the eighth great—Catherine Dubois, who lived in the little pioneer village of New Palz, New York, with her husband and infant daughter Sarah.

One day in 1663 a raiding party of Minnesink Indians descended from the Catskill Mountains and took Catherine and her infant daughter captive. Search parties from New Palz looked for them in vain for ten weeks. By that time, the Minnesinks were confident their prisoners wouldn't be rescued, so they proceeded to tie Catherine and baby Sarah to a pile of logs, intending the burn the two to death as a sacrifice. At this moment, Catherine began singing a hymn of praise. The Minnesinks were so fascinated that they began to demand a song—one after another. As her captors continued to force her to sing, there was just enough time for the village raiding party to burst upon the scene and rescue Catherine and Sarah.

One Thanksgiving Day, I brought my three boys and four of their cousins to a women's homeless shelter and they acted this story out in a skit to show the power of thanksgiving.

## WHY DO WE GIVE THANKS?

God is infinitely worthy of praise, and it is He who has declared praise and thanksgiving to be good.

It is good to give thanks to the Lord
And to sing praises to Your name, O Most High.
(Psalm 92:1)

Praise the Lord!
For it is good to sing praises to our God;
For it is pleasant and praise is becoming. (Psalm 147:1)

When we thank Him, we honor Him for who He is—the author of every good and perfect gift (Psalm 50:23; James 1:17).

Because God is infinitely good, our obedience to Him results in eternal benefits for His children. All of His commandments are for our eternal good (Deuteronomy 10:13). Here are just a few of the benefits that flow from the heart of God to His people who learn to praise and thank Him.

### Focuses our perspective on life

> Immediately the word concerning Nebuchadnezzar was fulfilled; and he was driven away from mankind and began eating grass like cattle, and his body was drenched with the dew of heaven until his hair had grown like eagles' feathers and his nails like birds' claws. But at the end of that period, I, Nebuchadnezzar, raised my eyes toward heaven and my reason returned to me, and I blessed the Most High and praised and honored Him who lives forever;
>
> For His dominion is an everlasting dominion,
> And His kingdom endures from generation to generation.
> (Daniel 4:33–34)

Thanking and praising God gives us a better perspective of life. When we lack this perspective we can envy the wicked who seem to be prospering while the godly suffer.[1] The regaining of a godly perspective will deliver us from this envy and remind us of the wonderful eternal glorious future for His children.[2] And thanksgiving will deliver us from pride because true thankfulness and praise is a recognition that every good and perfect gift comes from God.[3] The Scripture says that Nebuchadnezzar's reason returned to him when he acknowledged God as the sovereign of everything!

The deceit that we all battle is the illusion that we can find someone other than God who is worthy of our complete trust, admiration, and affection with no qualification. Praising God is a declaration that the search is over. Isn't it wonderful that "whoever believes in Him will not be disappointed" (Romans 10:11)?

## Replaces the inappropriate with thanks

> But immorality or any impurity or greed must not even be named among you, as is proper among saints; and there must be no filthiness and silly talk, or coarse jesting, which are not fitting, but rather giving of thanks. (Ephesians 5:3–4)

This passage illustrates the principle of replacement. The believer is not only told what to reject but also instructed to replace it with thanksgiving. Thanksgiving and praise is a way of occupying oneself with God and making Him the object of our confidence (Jeremiah 9:23–24). In this way one finds oneself beholding His glorious character, which is the means that the Spirit of God uses to transform our love. We become like the One upon whom we are focused (2 Corinthians 3:18). It is for this reason that thanksgiving is a necessary ingredient for replacing our anxiety with God's peace (Philippians 4:6–7)!

## Unifies relationships

> O magnify the Lord with me,
> And let us exalt His name together. (Psalm 34:3)

> Now may the God who gives perseverance and encouragement grant you to be of the same mind with one another according to Christ Jesus, so that with one accord you may with one voice glorify the God and Father of our Lord Jesus Christ. (Romans 15:5–6)

You cannot truly praise God with another if there is a barrier between you and someone else that needs reconciliation (Matthew 5:23–24). Our fleshy desire to draw attention to ourselves needs to be surrendered to the Holy Spirit who empowers us to draw attention to Christ (John 16:14).

## Leads to Guidance and Service

> While they were ministering to the Lord and fasting, the
> Holy Spirit said, "Set apart for Me Barnabas and Saul for the
> work to which I have called them." (Acts 13:2)

Our Lord connected worship and service in His declaration to Satan (Matthew 4:8–10). Whom we worship, we will serve. Anxiousness over our lack of direction can prompt us to praise God that He promises to be our Shepherd. When the sheep ends up in the right place, all praise goes to the Shepherd—not the sheep. According to Jeremiah 10:23, it does not lie within us to direct our paths. Take time at Thanksgiving to praise God that He will give you the direction you need in regard to the concerns of your hearts.

## PRAISE RELEASES THE POWER OF GOD

I know that God inhabits the praises of His people and responds to praise with His manifested presence (Psalm 22:3). We see this demonstrated in passages such as 2 Chronicles 20 and Acts 16:21–26.

It is wise for children to learn at the earliest age the great spiritual fruit of genuine thanksgiving and praise. If you celebrate with young children, let them act out the story of Catherine's and Sarah's deliverance from the Minnesink. Act out the story of Daniel 4 or 2 Chronicles 20. By doing so you are truly cultivating the spirit of thanksgiving and honoring our Lord on this day. We will further explore in the next chapter how to cultivate a habit of thanksgiving and praise.

NOTES

1. See Psalm 73.
2. Romans 8:18
3. James 1:17

Chapter
Ten

# Cultivating a *Spirit of Thanksgiving*

E lizabeth and Zacharias were a godly couple who had longed for and prayed to have a child of their own. Their desire went unfulfilled, and they were, in the words of Scripture, quite "advanced in years" (Luke 1:7).

One day an angel appeared to Zacharias, and after calming his fears announced that Elizabeth would have a son and that this son would bring joy to many people. When Zacharias responded by questioning and doubting the promise, God disciplined him by removing his ability to speak. When the baby was born Zacharias refused the suggestion of his neighbors and relatives to name the child after himself. Instead he obeyed God's guidance to name him John. At this moment as his ability to speak was restored to him, he began to praise God (Luke 1:64, 67–79)!

One way to develop a spirit of thanksgiving is to respond to the loving discipline of the Lord. In this way Zacharias's response illustrates the truth that "Praise is becoming to the upright" (Psalm 33:1). He was upright in responding to God's discipline.

## LIFE ON THE INSIDE

Thanksgiving is not something that we decide to "drum up" solely on our own initiative. One day in college I walked into a fraternity brother's room, and he began to share a little booklet with me about "How to be filled with the Spirit." I walked away from that encounter with the hope that there is a way to be a Christian on the "inside" and not merely on the outside. Outwardly my life was going great, but inwardly I was full of fear and anxiety. As I learned to open my life up to the Spirit's control, depend on His enablement for every responsibility, and respond to His leading and instruction in His word, my life was changed. Worship is the human response to the Spirit's initiative. No one can say, "Jesus is Lord" apart from the Holy Spirit (1 Corinthians 12:3). To be sure, a drunken man can mouth the words but only in the strength of God's Spirit can Christ control one's life (see Ephesians 3:16–17). As one is "filled with the Spirit" (5:18) the result is worship and thanksgiving (5:19–20)!

A number of years ago I organized my prayer life around a different emphasis each day. For example Monday was for missionaries, Friday was for family, and Tuesday was for Thanksgiving. When I first started this approach on Tuesday my well of thanksgiving did not seem to be as deep as my well of petitions the other days. What I discovered was that I needed to prime the pump! I would go through key passages of Scripture that spoke of spiritual blessing that the Lord had given to His children and use these verses as a springboard to aid my thanksgiving and praises. I providentially found Romans 5, 6, and 8 as well as Ephesians 1 to be helpful. Understanding your spiritual inheritance as a Christian is essential in cultivating a grateful heart. Realize that all that we have is due to God's grace.

## TWO THINGS ABOUT GOD

I once heard a godly young woman say that if you could believe two things about God you would have the necessary basis for continual gratitude. If God is sovereign and "works all things after the counsel of His will" (Ephesians 1:11), and if He is good and rules and overrules all things for the ultimate good of His people (Romans 8:28–29), then there is an objective basis to live a life of continual rejoicing, prayer, and thanksgiving (1 Thessalonians 5:16–18).

*Realize that all that we have is due to God's grace.*

At any moment—even this very moment—if any of us were getting what we have earned from our Creator we would be in a place of continual torment. Anything that any of us ever receives other than this is due to God's grace. We are not worthy of His lovingkindness and His gracious provisions (cf. Genesis 32:10).

The revelation of God's character is the main theme of Scripture, and the climax of this message is the person of Jesus Christ who is the radiance of God's glory and the exact representation of His nature (Hebrews 1:3). Meditation on His glorious character and His Spirit will transform your life (2 Corinthians 3:18). Thanksgiving is a glorious day if you use it to cultivate a spirit of thanksgiving for the coming year. Consider these ideas:

1. Follow Zacharias's example and respond to the Lord's loving discipline.

2. Invite the Spirit's control over all areas of your life and particular areas of your present struggles.

3. Plan a special time of thanksgiving and praise over a key passage of Scripture that tells you of your spiritual blessings.

4. Plan a time of praise and reflection on a particular attribute of God.

## WAITING ON GOD TO FULFILL HIS PROMISES AND SEEING HIM MEET YOUR NEEDS

Simeon was a man to whom God had made a promise that he would not die until he saw the Messiah (Luke 2:26). When Simeon came into the temple the day Mary and Joseph were dedicating the baby Jesus to the Lord, he took Him in his arms and blessed and praised God (Luke 2:27–28). Thank Him that He cares for you, and as you see Him work you will be drawn to praise and thank Him.

Seek the Lord at your point of concern and let God speak to you. The Bible is to be read with integrity in light of the context of the passage, and it is also to be read as a personal book. Every part of the Bible was not written to us but it was all written for us. How do you know when you can claim a promise? As stated earlier, you can look at the context and see what you have in common with the original audience. If a promise was given to Abraham you can note that you are not the father of the nation of Israel, but you, like him, are a child of God. If a promise was made to an apostle, you once again do not share a role in this capacity but you do

*Thank Him that He cares for you, and as you see Him work you will be drawn to praise and thank Him.*

share in the role of a child of God. In examining the promise you look at the analogy and Scripture to determine if the promise is universal or unique to a particular situation and not a general principle. For example, God promises to put the fear of God in the nation of Israel in a future time to restore them:

And I will give them one heart and one way, that they may fear Me always, for their own good and for the good of their children after them. I will make an everlasting covenant with them that I will not turn away from them, to do them good; and I will put the fear of Me in their hearts so that they will not turn away from Me. (Jeremiah 32:39–40)

Since God declares man's basic problem to be a lack of fear of God (Romans 3:18), and He commands every child of God to fear Him, a passage like Jeremiah 32:39–40 drives me to prayer to believe Him to put the fear of Him in my heart and my family. Allow me to illustrate this with a story from my own life.

After discovering the gracious provision of the Holy Spirit to live the Christian life, I surrendered my life to Him in 1972. Although I finished my college studies in Business, two years later, I sensed God's call to a vocational life of ministry. I entered seminary training after working under a godly pastor. During my first week of school God impressed my spirit with the truth of Proverbs 24:27:

Prepare your work outside
And make it ready for yourself in the field;
Afterwards, then, build your house.

In the Proverbs, to build one's house refers to marriage and rearing a family. This verse teaches that certain preparations are necessary before one builds their house. I sensed that God desired me to focus on the preparation side and forget about marriage as I pursued my studies. They lasted longer than anticipated because after a four-year program leading to a master's in theology, I entered a doctoral program.

When I completed my formal schooling and walked through the door that God had graciously opened to teach at Moody Bible Institute in Chicago, I reminded the Lord of Proverbs 24:27. Being twenty-eight and having finished my formal education, I asked the Lord, "Isn't it time to build my house?" God gave me eight and a half more years of singleness as I married my ministry of studying and teaching college students.

One day as I was praying about this area of my life I felt accused. These thoughts raced through my mind: "You're so idealistic. You're so unrealistic. You won't trust God to provide for you." When I was feeling so low that I desired to crawl under the rug in my apartment, Ephesians 3:20 popped into my mind:

Now to Him who is able to do far more abundantly beyond all that we ask or think, according to the power that works within us.

All I can say is that it answered those accusing thoughts. I did not take it in any specific way other than that I could trust God to do exceedingly abundantly beyond all I could ask or think in this area of my life. I carried around this word in my heart, and a number of years later when God sent Penny into my life I praised Him for His gracious provision. (The full story of this is in my book *Believing God for His Best: How to Marry Contentment and Singleness.*)

Seek the Lord and let Him speak to your need. What a wonderful thing to do at Thanksgiving! Thank Him that He cares for you, and as you see Him work you will be drawn to praise and thank Him.

These are a few suggestions that will make for both a happy and holy Thanksgiving celebration.

# PRACTICAL Help 12
## Scriptures to Aid the Discipline of Thanksgiving

Verses That Give Insight on Sacrifices That Believers Can Offer to God

Psalm 51:16–17; 141:2

Micah 6:6–8

Romans 12:1–2; 15:16

Philippians 4:18

Hebrews 13:15–16

I Peter 2:5

Revelation 5:8; 8:3–4

Verses That Give Insight into Unacceptable Worship

Exodus 32; 34:14

Leviticus 10:1–11

Deuteronomy 4:15–24

I Samuel 13:8–14

2 Samuel 6:1–9

Job 31:24–28

Isaiah 2:6–11; 48:11

Amos 5:21–27

Malachi 1:6–14; 3:13–15

Mark 7:6–7

Verses That Give Reasons to Praise God

Psalms 9:11-12; 63:3; 66:20; 68:19; 98:1-3; 103:1-5; 113; 119:164, 171; 139:17-18; 147; 148:5-6, 13; 149:4

Daniel 4:34-37

Romans 11:33-36; 16:25-27

2 Corinthians 1:3-5

Ephesians 1:3; 3:20-21

1 Peter 1:3

Jude 24-25

Revelation 4:8-11; 5:9-10; 7:10; 11:15-18; 15:3-4; 16:5, 7; 19:1-8

Verses That Give Reasons to Thank God

Psalms 7:17; 18:49-50; 118:1, 21, 28-29; 139:14-16

Acts 27:35

Romans 1:8

1 Corinthians 1:4-7

2 Corinthians 2:14; 4:15; 8:16; 9:12, 15

Philippians 1:3

Colossians 1:3; 3:17

1 Thessalonians 2:13; 5:18

1 Timothy 1:12-14

Verses That Give an Appropriate Perspective for Thanksgiving

Genesis 32:10

Job 1:20

Ecclesiastes 5:13-16

1 Timothy 6:5-10

James 1:17

# PRACTICAL Help 13

## Ideas to Enhance Your Thanksgiving Celebration

- Take out the past year's photos or most recent photo album and, as a family, thank God for His past acts of kindness, goodness, provisions, etc.

- Write down memories or events of the year as they occur and put them in a special box to be opened and the contents read around Thanksgiving.

- Buy or make cards and write thank-you notes, being sure to send them to those who might never receive a card or to those who wouldn't expect one.

- Make a Psalm 100 book by having young children write out or trace your letters line by line. Put one line per page and have children either draw or search through magazines, missionary newsletters, stickers, etc. for appropriate pictures that represent the concepts of the Psalm.

- Get a Psalter and learn one of the Praise Psalms together (Psalms 145–150).

- In early November, Penny would begin reading *Stories of the Pilgrims* by Margaret B. Pumphrey (published by Christian Liberty Press). It gives the full account of the trials the Pilgrims endured before coming to America, their wonderful convictions and resolve, and the Christian legacy of this country.

- Another effective tool is *The Pilgrims*, a delightful audio account of the Pilgrim journey distributed by The Children's Bible Club and read by "Aunt Carolyn." Listening with the children will provide a great opportunity to discuss the goodness, mercy, and sovereignty of God.

- Develop a Thanksgiving tradition. One of ours is after our Thanksgiving we visit the godly family where I (Bill) spent my Thanksgivings when I was single. It is a time of good, spiritual fellowship and concludes with an annual round-robin Ping-Pong game.

- Give a Thanksgiving quiz.
- Give a turkey quiz.

## Our Thanksgiving Quiz
### by Susan Dibble

How much do we really know about this most American of holidays? Take this Thanksgiving quiz to find out:

1. What year was the first Thanksgiving celebrated in the United States?
   a. 1492
   b. 1621
   c. 1776
   d. 1865

2. Who was one of the people who attended the first Thanksgiving feast?
   a. John Smith
   b. Pocahontas
   c. William Bradford
   d. Andrew Jackson

3. What food was definitely served when the Pilgrims feasted?
   a. turkey
   b. venison
   c. roast pig
   d. cranberries

4. Which Indian tribe joined the Pilgrims at that first feast?
   a. Iroquois
   b. Algonquin
   c. Wampanoag
   d. Potawatomi

5. How long did the first American Thanksgiving celebration last?
   a. one day
   b. three days
   c. one week
   d. one month

6. What famous American believed that the turkey, rather than the bald eagle, should be America's national bird?
   a. Thomas Jefferson
   b. Benjamin Franklin
   c. Henry David Thoreau
   d. Theodore Roosevelt

7. Which president issued the first national Thanksgiving proclamation?
   a. George Washington
   b. John Adams
   c. Abraham Lincoln
   d. Woodrow Wilson

8. Which president was the first to pardon a turkey?
   a. Abraham Lincoln
   b. Harry Truman
   c. John F. Kennedy
   d. Bill Clinton

9. Who helped establish Thanksgiving as a national holiday?
   a. Abigail Adams
   b. Betsy Ross
   c. Harriet Beecher Stowe
   d. Sarah Josepha Hale

10. How many feathers does a mature turkey have?
   a. 1,000
   b. 3,500
   c. 10,000
   d. one million

II. What food is not native to America?
    a. turkey
    b. pumpkins
    c. corn
    d. apples

12. What percentage of American families eat turkey
    for Thanksgiving?
    a. 90 percent
    b. 75 percent
    c. 60 percent
    d. 55 percent

13. How much did the heaviest turkey ever raised weigh?
    a. 50 pounds
    b. 66 pounds
    c. 86 pounds
    d. 105 pounds

14. How fast can turkeys fly?
    a. 20 mph
    b. 40 mph
    c. 55 mph
    d. turkeys can't fly

15. What sound does a female turkey make?
    a. *gobble, gobble*
    b. *click, click*
    c. *coo, coo*
    d. male turkeys rule the roost and the females remain
       silent

16. The wild turkey is native to what area of the world?
    a. northern Mexico and eastern United States
    b. Canada
    c. northern Europe
    d. China

17. Illinois is the top producer of what food associated with Thanksgiving?
    a. corn
    b. turkey
    c. pumpkins
    d. sweet potatoes

18. In what country is the most turkey consumed per capita?
    a. United States
    b. Great Britain
    c. Spain
    d. Israel

19. Since what year has football been associated with Thanksgiving?
    a. 1874
    b. 1900
    c. 1934
    d. 1952

20. Some American Indians mark Thanksgiving with a National Day of Mourning. What was the first year it was held?
    a. 1750
    b. 1890
    c. 1970
    d. 1985

## Answers

1. (b) The first American Thanksgiving was celebrated in 1621 by Plymouth Colony to commemorate the harvest after a harsh winter. It was a traditional English harvest feast.

2. (c) William Bradford, the governor of Plymouth Colony, proclaimed the Thanksgiving feast and was one of 53 Pilgrims who attended.

3. (b) The only specific food recorded was the five deer brought by the Indians. Wild turkey was plentiful and may have been served.

4. (c) About 90 Wampanoag Indians attended.

5. (b) The celebration lasted three days.

6. (b) Comparing the turkey to the eagle, Benjamin Franklin wrote, "The turkey is a much more respectable bird, and withal a true native of America."

7. (a) George Washington issued the first Presidential Thanksgiving Proclamation in 1789.

8. (a) Abraham Lincoln's son, Tad, had befriended a turkey named Jack that Lincoln pardoned to save him from becoming the White House Christmas dinner. The pardoning of a Thanksgiving turkey became a presidential tradition in 1947 with Harry Truman.

9. (d) Sarah Josepha Hale, editor of the widely read *Godey's Lady's Book*, crusaded for years to establish a national Thanksgiving day, rather than have individual states celebrate their own. Hale's campaign bore fruit when Abraham Lincoln issued Thanksgiving proclamations in 1863 and 1864.

10. (b) Mature turkeys have 3,500 feathers.

11. (d) Apples are not native to North America.

12. (a) Ninety percent is the most commonly cited figure.

13. (c) The heaviest turkey ever raised weighed 86 pounds.

14. Trick question. Wild turkeys can fly up to 55 mph for short distances. Domesticated turkeys are bred to have such heavy breasts they cannot fly—or mate without human intervention.

15. (b) The male turkeys are the gobblers.

16. (a) This native bird was first domesticated in Mexico and Central America. Spain imported it to Europe, where it was considered a dish fit for kings.

17. (c) Illinois is the top pumpkin producer.

18. (d) Israel, where annual consumption is 28 lbs. per person.

19. (a) The first football game was played on Thanksgiving in
    1874. The NFL tradition is often associated with the 1934
    game played between the Detroit Lions and Chicago
    Bears. The Bears won, but playing football on Thanksgiv-
    ing Day became firmly established in Detroit.

20. (c) The National Day of Mourning started in 1970 when a
    Wampanoag leader delivered a speech on Coles Hill, over-
    looking Plymouth Rock.

Sources: the Pilgrim Hall Museum in Plymouth, Mass.; the University of
Illinois Extension; Penelope Bingham, a member of the Illinois Humani-
ties Council; Illinois Corn Growers Association; and websites for the Pro
Football Hall of Fame, SportsJones and Ezine articles.

## TURKEY QUIZ

1. What is the name of the skin that hangs off the turkey's
   neck?
   a. wattle
   b. snark
   c. gobbler

2. What are male turkeys called?
   a. toms
   b. bobs
   c. harrys

3. How fast can a turkey trot?
   a. 15 mph
   b. 25 mph
   c. 40 mph

4. What name have anti-Pilgrim protesters given to Thanksgiving?
   a. Judgment Day
   b. The European Invasion
   c. National Day of Mourning

5. According to the Butterball Co., how much turkey is
   served on Thanksgiving?
   a. 500,000 pounds
   b. 100 million pounds
   c. 675 million pounds

## Answers

1. a; 2. a; 3. b; 4. c; 5. c

Source: www.infoplease.com

# Section Five
*Christmas*

Chapter Eleven

# Welcoming the Lord to Your *Home for the Holidays*

Much has been said about the little story at the end of Luke chapter 10. It is a five-verse account of Christ coming to the home of Martha and Mary. This is a tale of two sisters, and for many Martha is the perfect hostess. She is concerned about every detail and desires everything to be done just right.

Luke 10:38–42 is not technically a story about Christmas, but it provides us with some helpful insight into celebrating this holiday. The phrase at the beginning of verse 40 sounds like Christmas to me: "But Martha was *distracted* with all her preparations." I would like us to first concentrate on what Martha did *right*! Martha welcomed Christ into her home.

## BEGINNING THE SEASON RIGHT

The record of Martha welcoming Christ into her home is the inspiration for a special Christmas tradition in our family. At the beginning of December, our family has a special dinner. We use our best dishes and look forward to this annual event. On this occasion we set an extra place setting at the table for our Lord. It is at the end of the table because He is both the Head and the Special Guest at this meal.

As we enjoy our meal, our dinner conversation is directed to our unseen Guest. We welcome Him to our holiday celebration and share our excitement with Him of celebrating His birth into our world. It is a time when we share our plans as well as ask for His ideas for the holidays. Most of all we tell that we desire Him to both rule and overrule our agenda so that He truly is the honored guest of every aspect of our Christmas celebrations.

The empty chair and beautiful place setting are vivid reminders of our Lord's presence with us that evening. All of us seek to share our hearts with Christ that night. One year my wife told Him in tears how hard it was going to be to celebrate Christmas for the first time without her father who had gone to be with his Savior in June. Christ gave me the idea, and I shared with Him that night how we desired to honor Penny's dad that Christmas. While Dr.

Bauer was no longer with us physically, we desired to let everyone express special memories of him and their gratitude for the spiritual legacy he gave. The Lord was once again showing us that He—the unseen Guest—was the greatest reality at the table that night. He was showing us that He understood our circumstances and desired to aid us in our celebrations of this holiday.

It was a joy that Christmas season to honor the man who had been my father through marriage and the grandfather of our children. He had been gloriously saved while in combat in World War Two. As his plane was under attack, he called upon the Lord, and God heard his cry. It proved not to be just a mere teary and emotional plea for help but one that commenced a lifelong relationship with Christ. He, like all of us, was not perfect, but he did exhibit a peaceful and faithful spirit as he sought to serve his family. All who knew him certainly witnessed his generous and accepting spirit.

*"My greatest joy was trusting Christ as my Savior, but I do not believe I have had any disappointment." I was a little puzzled . . .*

At his eightieth birthday party, which turned out to be his final one, was a planned question-and-answer time that we recorded on video. My wife would later put them on three DVDs and give them as Christmas gifts to her sister and two brothers. One of the questions was asked by our son David, the youngest grandchild. "Grandfather, what was your greatest joy and your greatest disappointment in life?" He replied, "My greatest joy was trusting Christ as my Savior, but I do not believe I have had any disappointment."

I was a little puzzled, because in the time that I had known him I knew of some setbacks he had experienced. His inventor-mind had produced numerous ideas that could have potentially made him an extremely wealthy man, but this did not materialize. He never lacked, but he died living only on social security. His *contentment* in this state was a richer heritage than millions of dollars! I believe his realization of this was the reason for his not being disappointed. We trace the idea of honoring this godly man and edifying the extended family to that particular night of welcoming Jesus to our home for the holidays.

Perhaps you have had a death or disappointment this past year that's casting a shadow over your Christmastime. You might want to purposefully remember a loved one in a significant way. And if your disappointment has been of a different nature, be open about it with the Lord. Ask Him to show you how you can welcome His Son to your home in a special way during this season.

## NOT ONLY THE 25th

As a family, we also carve out a day before December 25 to celebrate our personal, family Christmas. We begin with our boys coming down the stairs to Handel's *Messiah*. Then we proceed to read one of the great New Testament passages about the person of Christ—John 1, Colossians 1, Hebrews 1, or Philippians 2. We open our gifts and enjoy a leisurely day that is void of any outside expectations or pressures. This enables us to host the Christmas dinner with a focus on our guests and without the pressure of trying to fit in our own personal Christmas.

You may use another tradition, but whatever it is, do not forget to invite Jesus to it. Yes, we can all imitate Martha in welcoming Christ at our home for Christmas and for all our holiday celebrations. The next chapter will guide us in avoiding her mistake that robbed her of the joy of Christ's visit.

Chapter Twelve

# Enjoying the *Lord in the Holidays*

What would it be like to know you have the most glorious plans and agenda for your holidays? Martha's plan to invite Christ to her home was unquestionably the best plan one could ever have. What is notable is the fact that she did not enjoy the visit!

Why did our loving Lord counsel His diligent hostess? It was not because of her serving or her hard work. If we just look quickly over the account in Luke 10:38–42 we might conclude that Jesus is praising Mary for being passive and rebuking Martha for her diligence. This is certainly not the case. There was nothing wrong with what Martha was doing. What was wrong was the attitude that undergirded her work.

Jesus could not commend Martha's service because it was a service that distracted her from enjoying the Lord. It was a service that was characterized by being worried and bothered about so many details. Such service is not motivated by trusting the Lord with the burden of the work, and without this faithful trusting "it is impossible to please God" (Hebrews 11:6).

## WHEN THERE'S SO MUCH TO DO

When you feel responsible for the success of an event, a ministry, or any kind of undertaking—including preparations for Christmas—it is more difficult to enjoy the Lord through the process. It is more natural to occupy yourself with the details of the project rather than being occupied with the Lord. Such a mind-set does distract us and lead to worry.

The Lord loves you in your anxious state. He is not pleased with it, and that is true evidence of His love for us. He loves us when we are frazzled and have taken upon ourselves responsibilities that He has asked us to cast upon Him as 1 Peter 5:7 reminds us to cast "all your anxiety on Him, because He cares for you."

Yes, He loves, but He loves us so much that He has not sentenced us to live that way. He died for us that we could not only be forgiven but also freed to experience a life of fellowship with

*Have you* cast *all the burdens of your holiday plans on the Lord?*

Himself and enjoy His peace in the midst of the demands of life.

Why does our Lord lovingly counsel Martha? Once again, it was not because of her actions per se but the attitude and drive behind them that was not characterized by faith. Her zeal to do right had unconsciously tempted her to take matters into her own hands. The motivation behind our Lord's word to her was His great love, which reflects His discerning insight into the results of this type of service.

## YES, HE CARES!

What is the trait of the attitude that we observe in Martha? It is revealed in her words to our Lord. "Lord, do you *not care* . . ." (Luke 10:40). This attitude leads to *doubt* in God's goodness and care. When we are doubting God's care for us, it is probable evidence that we are carrying a burden that He has not asked us to carry. Have you *cast* all the burdens of your holiday plans on the Lord? We are not to be ignorant of Satan's schemes (2 Corinthians 2:11), and his most basic scheme is to promote doubt in God's goodness. Such doubt is what plunged man into a life of independence from God.

Martha continues, "Lord, do not you care that my sister has *left* me to do all the serving *alone*?" The fruit of this attitude leaves us feeling *abandoned* and *alone* with all the burden of the work on our shoulders. In a practical sense, you may be the one who is doing the bulk of the work, which is why a major holiday adds to the everyday stress. For this reason, many women tend to identify with Martha and feel she gets a bum rap in the retelling of this story. As you talk this over with the Lord, ask for His wisdom and strength to organize Christmas: What needs to be done? When?

Who will do it? This way one person needn't feel that she's responsible for all preparations. As we walk openly, honestly, and transparently before the Lord, our feeling of being alone can be met by His fellowship and His cleansing:

> But if we walk in the Light as He Himself is in the Light, we have fellowship with one another, and the blood of Jesus His Son cleanses us from all sin. (1 John 1:7)

After a speaker poured out his heart all week at a church's special services and yet saw very little result, a breakthrough came on a Sunday morning. Usually the pastor invited people to share prayer requests at the beginning of the morning service. On that day, one person asked to come to the front and share his burden. He openly confessed his resentment of feeling that all the work of the church was being placed on him and exhibited a great brokenness over his sinful attitude.

This honest sharing became contagious and spread through the congregation. One by one people came forward and shared with their congregation their burdens and appropriately confessed their sin. The pastor or the guest speaker did not try to prolong it and even sought to bring it to a close several times. This work of the Spirit could not be stopped that morning but lasted until almost three o'clock in the afternoon even though a potluck lunch had been scheduled at the church at noon. When you are feeling alone and burdened you need to obey the advice of Hebrews 4:16:

> Therefore let us draw near with confidence to the throne of grace, so that we may receive mercy and find grace to help in time of need.

God desires to respond to you in merciful compassion and to give you His grace for any part of your holiday plans.

Another fruit of Martha's attitude is seen in her words, "Then tell her to help me." After expressing her doubt of His care for her and her feeling alone in the burden of the work, she reveals her demanding attitude. When the conscious or unconscious demands of our soul begin to treat Christ as our servant rather than our Master, many conflicts will occur. Only as we are under God's authority are we able to experience victory in the warfare that surrounds our life and our holiday celebration.

*A point of pride is any area of my life where I am resisting God.*

Submit therefore to God. Resist the devil and he will flee from you. (James 4:7)

Use the battle to let the Lord draw you into a deeper surrender of yourself and all the details of the occasion to Him. Our own desires—even the desire to serve Christ or our family in a certain way—can easily replace Christ as the practical driving force in our life. When this happens, we have conflicts with anyone whom we sense comes between us and our desire being fulfilled.

This demanding attitude "Then tell her to help me" also is an example of pride that God opposes (James 4:6).

A point of pride is any area of my life where I am resisting God. God honors repentance of this resistance and desires to draw near to us (James 4:8). As we humble ourselves before Him, He can give us the grace (motivation and enablement) for every demand of our life during the holiday season.

God lovingly counseled Martha, and He will graciously counsel and discipline us. The motivation for His action is His great *love* for us to avoid the bitter fruit of Martha's mistake. Why not surrender to His love this Christmas?

Chapter
Thirteen

Making the
*Right Choice*
*in the*
*Holidays*

How can one enjoy Christ during the Christmas holidays? Martha invited Christ to her home but did not have time to enjoy His visit. If Christ is to be the center of your holiday celebrations, how can we learn to enjoy Him?

Martha's sister Mary took a seat at the Lord's feet and listened to His word (Luke 10:39). Mary's action is contrasted with the distracted spirit of Martha. Our Lord commends her for choosing "the *good* part" (Luke 10:42).

## STAYING CLOSE TO CHRIST

Mary's action is what Jesus would term *abiding in the Lord* (John 15). It is the life that Jesus exemplified in His relationship with the Father. His pattern of life is to be imitated as we see in1 John 2:6:

The one who says he abides in Him ought himself to walk in the same manner as He walked.

Christ certainly intimately understood the pressure that Martha was feeling but perfectly exemplified what He commended in Mary. Consider the busyness that could have overwhelmed Jesus as you meditate on these truths as written in Helmut Thielicke's lyrical description of Christ from *The Waiting Father*:

What tremendous pressures there must have been within him to drive him to hectic, nervous, explosive activity! He sees . . . as no one else ever sees, with an infinite and awful nearness, the agony of the dying man, the prisoner's torment, the anguish of the wounded conscience, injustice, terror, dread, and beastliness. He sees and hears and feels all this with the heart of a Savior. . . . Must not this fill every waking hour and rob him of sleep at night? Must he not begin immediately to set the fire burning, to win people, to work out strategic plans to evangelize the world, to work, work, furiously work, unceasingly, unrestingly, before the night comes when no man can work? That's what we could imagine the earthly life of the Son of God would be like, if we were to think of him in human terms.

But how utterly different was the actual life of Jesus! Though the burden of the whole world lay heavy upon his shoulders, though Corinth and Ephesus and Athens, whole continents, with all their desperate need, were dreadfully near to his heart, though suffering and sinning were going on in chamber, street corner, castle, and slums, seen only by the Son of God—though this immeasurable misery and wretchedness cried aloud for a physician, he has time to stop and talk to the individual. . . .

By being obedient in his little corner of the highly provincial precincts of Nazareth and Bethlehem he allows himself to be fitted into a great mosaic whose master is God. And that's why he has time for people; for all time is in the hands of his Father. And that too is why peace and not unrest goes out from him, For God's faithfulness already spans the world like a rainbow; he does not need to build; he needs only to walk beneath it.

## HUSHED, NOT RUSHED

I have a special memory of a day that the Lord slowed me down in an unusual way. Dr. George Sweeting, the president of Moody Bible Institute at that time, was so moved by the chapel speaker that he announced that classes were to be canceled the next day—they were to meet but only to pray. With that one announcement my responsibility of preparing and teaching for several hours was eliminated. It was a gift of God.

As I sought the Lord about how to use this day I sensed the need to put down all my normal disciplines and even speak as few words as I possibly could. I went to my classes, and after a few simple instructions, I joined the students in prayer. At the end of the day I, being single at the time, walked into a restaurant and ordered a

meal. A server said something interesting to me: "I go all over this
restaurant and I sense hurry
and rush, but I came to your
booth and I sense peace."
She said it not once or even
twice but three times! If you
had asked me, "What did
you do today?" I could have
replied, "Not much of anything." However, God desired to
show me that when He orders one to
slow down, be quiet, and seek Him, it can bear great fruit.

> *I sensed the need to put down all my normal disciplines and even speak as few words as I possibly could.*

## AT HIS FEET

The attitude of Mary is one of truth and loving devotion. As
she sat at the Lord's feet she was willing to do anything He would
ask of her. True faith always involves a genuine submission of
one's will to Christ's. It also reflects a complete trust in His care
of us and His ability to provide for us and direct us.

This faith that is the driving force behind Mary's ability to
enjoy the Lord is the antithesis of fear. This freedom from fear is
based on the fact that God will not and cannot fail us. This is the
clear principle you can see in the Lord's comforting words to Israel
in Isaiah 46:3–4:

> Listen to Me, O house of Jacob,
> And all the remnant of the house of Israel,
> You who have been borne by Me from birth
> And have been carried from the womb;
> Even to your old age I shall be the same,
> And even to your graying years I shall bear you!
> I have done it, and I shall carry you;
> And I shall bear you and I shall deliver you.

Just as God cared for His people from birth when they were fully helpless, so will He care for you. He promised to provide this same care throughout our lives—even in our older years when we might once again be as helpless as a little baby! He had done it and pledged to do it in the future. We do not have to fear. God will not fail us! When this truth lodges into your spirit, you can begin to abide in the Lord.

The Lord commends Mary for choosing "the good part which shall not be taken away from her" (Luke 10:42). It produces works of eternal value, and the failure to abide in the Lord produces a life of vanity. Take some time every day to dwell on these words:

> I am the vine, you are the branches; he who abides in Me and I in him, he bears much fruit, for apart from Me you can do nothing. (John 15:5)

You will see that you need Him in order to accomplish what He calls you to do, and you *will* bear much fruit if you abide in Him!

The section of Scripture that precedes (Luke 10:25–37) and the section of Scripture that follows (Luke 11:1–13) this little story are not chronologically related to it. In other words, their inspired placement is not chronological but thematic. The study of the Good Samaritan precedes the Lord's word to Mary and Martha and the account of the Lord's teaching on prayer follows it. The anxious and hurried spirit of Martha chokes out the spontaneous compassion that is seen in the Good Samaritan and a hurried spirit is the death of true prayer. On the other hand, the attitude of Mary is what allows for spontaneous love and also communion with God in prayer. What the Lord commends in Mary is the secret to a spiritually fruitful Christmas.

Chapter
Fourteen

Enhancing Your
*Relationship
with Christ
in the Holidays*

G iven the spiritual pressure of the holiday, it is important to go on the offensive and actively trust God to enhance your relationship with Him. If you have a better relationship with the Lord at the end of the holiday celebrations, you have had a very successful holiday.

## SOMETHING TO CELEBRATE

Preparing for the holiday can be so hectic that you can forget what life is all about. To discover the purpose of life we need to go to God's revelation to us—the Bible. One might ask, "How could somebody like me really understand this volume of sixty-six books in a way that I could really have a sense of purpose in the midst of all the struggles of my hectic life?"

Would it help to know that the message of the Bible is really the answer to one simple question—"What is God like?" God has disclosed Himself to us, and the supreme and climatic revelation was in the person of Jesus Christ who "is the *image* of the invisible God" (Colossians 1:15) and "the radiance of [God's] glory" (Hebrews 1:3).

The believer is not to be ignorant of Satan's schemes (2 Corinthians 2:11), and his most basic scheme is to distort your understanding of God. This is in harmony with the fact that his very name "Satan" means "adversary." He actively opposes God's purposes and demonstrated his deceitful character in his first encounter with mankind in Genesis 3:1–5. When Adam and Eve believed Satan's lie about God not being absolutely faithful and true ("You will surely not die") and not really good ("God knows that in the day you eat from it your eyes will be opened"),

*God knows the emptiness and pressure of living independently of Himself.*

they acted in pride (independence of God) and idolatry (looking to the forbidden fruit to meet the thirst of their heart). When we act independently of God—which is pride—and look to something or someone other than God to meet the thirst of our heart, we are following Satan's scheme. Anytime we follow his scheme, the result is always *vanity*.

Unless the Lord builds the house,
They labor in *vain* who build it;
Unless the Lord guards the city,
The watchman keeps awake in *vain*.
It is *vain* for you to rise up early,
To retire late,
To eat the bread of painful labors;
For He gives to His beloved even in his sleep.
(Psalm 127:1–2)

I am the vine, you are the branches; he who abides in Me and I in him, he bears much fruit, for apart from Me you can do nothing. (John 15:5)

## THE TRUE PURPOSE OF LIFE

God knows the emptiness and pressure of living independently of Himself. If we take life into our own hands for the holiday, it is up to us to carry our burdens on our own shoulders and to figure out what is best apart from the wisdom of God. Christ came to deliver us out of this vain way of life and to bring us into a relationship with God. When we turn to God from whatever idol we have trusted to meet our needs, we are given the gift of "life."

This is eternal life, that they may know You, the only true God, and Jesus Christ whom You have sent.
(John 17:3)

The purpose of life is found in comprehending and knowing God:

> Thus says the Lord, "Let not a wise man boast of his wisdom, and let not the mighty man boast of his might, let not a rich man boast of his riches; but let him who boasts boast of this, that he understands and knows Me, that I am the Lord who exercises lovingkindness, justice and righteousness on earth; for I delight in these things," declares the Lord. (Jeremiah 9:23–24)

To comprehend God is to understand that He is loving, trustworthy, and delightful. To know Him is to respond to our understanding and love, trust, and delight in our present experience.

As you trust God to enhance your relationship with Him during the holiday, you can let Him remind you that this is the purpose of "life." Use the holiday as a time to look to Him to remind you of His great love for you. The Father's affirmation of Jesus at His baptism, "This is my beloved Son in whom I am well-pleased" (Matthew 3:17) is also His attitude toward His people. Every believer is spiritually in Christ, and we should remember that the Father loves us as believers with the same intensity with which He loves His own Son (John 17:23). Look up this verse and pray its truth into your life.

*As you develop your relationship with Him, you are achieving something eternally significant.*

What burdens does the Lord desire you to trust Him with this Christmas? As you let Him understand you and carry your burdens, you are fulfilling His purpose and design for you. As you develop your relationship with Him, you are achieving something eternally significant. May God abundantly bless your relationship with Him this Christmas!

Chapter
Fifteen

Trusting in God
for Rest and
*Refreshment
in the Holidays*

Following four years of college and four more years of graduate school, I found myself in a state of exhaustion—physically, mentally, and emotionally, and even spiritually. As a kind and gracious answer to prayer, the Lord provided an inexpensive standby flight from Dallas, Texas, to London, England, where I could visit a good friend for two weeks, who was studying at Manchester University. We walked the countryside of northern England, enjoyed each other's fellowship, and ate his wife's good cooking. It was a delightful time as I experienced Psalm 23:2–3. The Lord did restore my soul!

## PASTURES AND DESERTS

The Scripture says that the shepherd "makes me lie down." In Hebrew grammar, the stem of the verb in Psalm 23:2 carries this causative nuance as does the stem of "He leads me" in the same verse. This conveys the truth that God is the initiator, and it is His wise guidance that leads the sheep.

The "green pastures" are in contrast to the barren desert where the sheep can so easily wander. In the same way, we as believers can tend to get distracted by the barren deserts of the world in our attempt to meet our needs during a holiday for rest and refreshment. Our culture has determined to pay any price to be entertained in order to fill an empty heart that is thirsting for Christ's love, peace, and joy.

The "quiet waters" meet the sheep's need for its thirst as well as its need for cleansing. They are in contrast to the rapid currents that could easily drown the sheep, who are poor swimmers, and dash their bodies against the sharp rocks. For this reason the shepherd takes some rocks and dams up a small body of water to provide the "quiet waters" to meet the needs of his flock. A believer can also suffer great disaster in trying to meet his thirsts when he is allured by the rushing waves of the world. We are encouraged to look to Christ and let Him satisfy us.

The phrase "He restores my soul" (Psalm 23:3a) is a summary and explanation of the two phrases of 23:2 discussed in the previous two paragraphs. Christ is willing and able to quicken the exhausted spirit as he did for me in England. He even led me through literal walks of green pastures, and on one occasion a still body of water was in the middle of the pasture. I have just come through a Christmas holiday where I trusted God for restful restoration for my life and my family, and He has been faithful to provide it. A sheep only fully rests when he is full and satisfied. Let Him minister to you in your hurt, which can so easily turn to anger, and your fears and guilt, which can destroy a sense of rest.[1]

*We are encouraged to look to Christ and let Him satisfy us.*

Christ knows who you are and what you need. Pray in faith that He would fully restore your soul and give you rest and refreshment this holiday—whatever your circumstances may be.

## IT'S OKAY TO REST!

As you look to Christ to rest and refresh you, open every facet of your being to His control. You are a spiritual person, but you also live in a physical body. There are times when the most spiritual thing you can do is to eat a good meal and get a good night's sleep. As you do a spiritual checkup, make sure that you are not ignoring the Sabbath principle. I have discovered I can get more done in six days than in seven as I have learned to rest and enjoy the change of pace that God our Creator designed us to have.

During your holiday you can look to God to both refresh you with people as well as with solitude. Godly people can be a source of refreshment.

For I have come to have much joy and comfort in your love, because the hearts of the saints have been refreshed through you, brother. (Philemon 7)

There are also times when the demands of life have been so much that you may be in need of solitude to recharge your batteries. Our Lord recognized and practiced this for Himself.

In the early morning, while it was still dark, Jesus got up, left the house, and went away to a secluded place, and was praying there. (Mark 1:35)

He also encouraged His followers to do the same.

And He said to them, "Come away by yourselves to a secluded place and rest a while." (For there were many people coming and going, and they did not even have time to eat.) (Mark 6:31)

Sometimes the most unselfish thing you can do is to minister to yourself and replenish your emotional resources.

The wonderful thing is that the Lord knows you, your unique personality, your unique needs, and your unique circumstances. It is restful in itself to know that you have One Person to ultimately please (Galatians 1:10) and One Master to ultimately serve (Matthew 6:24). Trust Him and Him alone to "make glad your soul" this Christmas holiday!

Make glad the soul of Your servant,
For to You, O Lord, I lift up my soul.
For You, Lord, are good, and ready to forgive,
And abundant in lovingkindness to all who call upon You.
(Psalm 86:4–5)

## PENNY'S Thoughts

So much has been written about how to celebrate Christmas that it can be overwhelming! The key in my life has been to plan way ahead in gift purchasing and to stay as rested as possible during this busy season. Rest has been key in helping me to be sensitive to the Holy Spirit's leading in reaching out to others and encouraging a joyful, peaceful, worshipful atmosphere in our home. Believe me, I've not always been successful; the full calendar can easily become a heavy burden instead of the joyous celebration of Christ's emptying Himself to live a perfect life among us.

May this not be true of our homes! May God grant us His wisdom and grace to walk in the preordained good works He has for us. Below are some tools and ways that have helped to keep my mind and heart focused on Jesus.

- Play beautiful, peaceful, Christ-centered Christmas music often. Handel's *Messiah* is one of our favorites.
- Read *My First Story of Christmas* by Tim Dowley to young children.
- *A Family Christmas Treasury* by Adrian Rogers is a wonderful little book that has a reading for each day of December centering on the person of Jesus Christ.
- Get George Sarris's CD on *The Life of Christ*. This CD contains dramatic readings word for word from the Bible. One section is from Luke 2. Children can easily memorize this passage with repeated listening.
- Use advent calendars that have Scriptures with the pictures.
- Pray about how God would want to use you and your family to love His world for His glory. Be open to new ideas (not so steeped in tradition that there is no room to respond to God's promptings). This is the key, isn't it?

God has a work He wants to do; we need to be listening and available with a loving and humble spirit.

NOTE

1. In my book *How to Be a Soul Physician: Learning How Christ Meets the Deepest Longings of a Soul through the Grace of Prayer* (Morelia, Mexico: Berea Publishers, 2010), I have developed the topics of guilt, fear, and anger.

Chapter Sixteen

Learning to Be a Channel of *God's Love in the Holidays*

Many have taken Isaiah 14 to not only refer to the king of Babylon but also a reference to Satan who energized the ruler, just as Satan is behind the reference to the serpent in Genesis 3. The five "I wills" of Isaiah 14:13–14 reveal his self-seeking spirit that has poisoned all of humanity.

Holidays can be a self-seeking time that is an antithesis to the life of our Lord who "did not come to be served, but to serve, and to give His life a ransom for many" (Matthew 20:28).

Any attempt to honor Christ in a holiday should include asking how He desires to use you as a channel of His love.

## IT'S BLESSED TO GIVE AND RECEIVE

There is a difference between simply doing acts of service and being a channel of Christ's love. The former can be done in the spirit of accomplishing a spiritual checklist and in an attitude of superiority and pride. A friend of mine spends time shopping for and serving a ninety-year-old woman and her handicapped son. The service took a new meaning when he said he began serving with an attitude of being willing to not only give but also to learn from her. Even the apostle Paul spoke of ministry as being a two-way street.

For I long to see you so that I may impart some spiritual gift to you, that you may be established; that is, that I may be encouraged together with you while among you, each of us by the other's faith, both yours and mine. (Romans 1:11–12)

He sought to not only encourage them but was encouraged by their faith as well.

Holidays are a time to trust the Lord for His plans. God is kind—even kind to evil and ungrateful people (Luke 6:35)! He desires His people to experience and express His love. Talk to Him about your family members, friends, or other people in need. Do not neglect to consider those that the Lord takes special delight

*Being a vessel of love during any holiday celebration can certainly take a lot of different forms.*

in—widows, orphans, and others in special need.

God may lay on your heart to partner with a missionary organization that aids some of these special people. One highlight one Christmas was taking a refugee family shopping. On a few occasions our family, along with others, has arranged to go to a nursing home on Christmas day to put on a simple service. People who are left alone at a nursing home on Christmas day are truly alone. God has good works that He has planned for each of us.

For we are His workmanship, created in Christ Jesus for good works, which God prepared beforehand so that we would walk in them. (Ephesians 2:10)

He does not expect all of us to do the same things or necessarily the same things each holiday or even each year but simply to be available to Him to fulfill His loving plans.

## A TIMELESS TREASURE

Here's a great story about one family's Christmas tradition. I hope you benefit from it as much as I have.

### The White Envelope[1]

It's just a small, white envelope stuck among the branches of our Christmas tree. No name, no identification, no inscription. It has peeked through the branches of our tree for the past ten years or so.

It all began because my husband, Mike, hated Christmas—

oh, not the true meaning of Christmas, but the commercial aspects of it: overspending; the frantic running around at the last minute to get a tie for Uncle Harry and the dusting powder for Grandma; the gifts given in desperation because you couldn't think of anything else.

Knowing he felt this way, I decided one year to bypass the usual shirts, sweaters, ties, and so forth. I reached for something special just for Mike. The inspiration came in an unusual way.

Our son Kevin, who was twelve that year, was wrestling at the junior level at the school he attended, and shortly before Christmas, there was a non-league match against a team sponsored by an inner-city church. These youngsters, dressed in sneakers so ragged that shoestrings seemed to be the only thing holding them together, presented a sharp contrast to our boys in their spiffy blue and gold uniforms and sparkling new wrestling shoes. As the match began, I was alarmed to see that the other team was wrestling without headgear, a kind of light helmet designed to protect a wrestler's ears.

It was a luxury the ragtag team obviously could not afford. Well, we ended up walloping them. We took every weight class. And as each of their boys got up from the mat, he swaggered around in his tatters with false bravado, a kind of street pride that couldn't acknowledge defeat.

Mike, seated beside me, shook his head sadly. "I wish just one of them could have won," he said. "They have a lot of potential, but losing like this could take the heart right out of them."

Mike loved kids—all kids—and he knew them, having coached Little League, football, baseball, and lacrosse. That's when the idea for his present came.

That afternoon, I went to a local sporting goods store and bought an assortment of wrestling headgear and shoes and sent them anonymously to the inner-city church. On Christmas

Eve, I placed the envelope on the tree, the note inside telling Mike what I had done and that this was his gift from me. His smile was the brightest thing about Christmas that year and in succeeding years. For each Christmas, I followed the tradition— one year sending a group of mentally handicapped youngsters to a hockey game, another year a check to a pair of elderly brothers whose home had burned to the ground the week before Christmas, and on and on.

The envelope became the highlight of our Christmas. It was always the last thing opened on Christmas morning and our children, ignoring their new toys, would stand with wide-eyed anticipation as their dad lifted the envelope from the tree to reveal its contents.

As the children grew, the toys gave way to more practical presents, but the envelope never lost its allure. The story doesn't end there.

You see, we lost Mike last year due to dreaded cancer. When Christmas rolled around, I was still so wrapped in grief that I barely got the tree up. But Christmas Eve found me placing an envelope on the tree, and in the morning, it was joined by three more. Each of our children, unbeknownst to the others, had placed an envelope on the tree for their dad. The tradition has grown and someday will expand even further with our grandchildren standing around the tree with wide-eyed anticipation watching as their fathers take down the envelope.

Mike's spirit, like the Christmas spirit, will always be with us.

This story was the inspiration for us to start a family tradition of each person giving a gift to Jesus for Christmas. This is my highlight of the gifts given or received at Christmas in our family. I remember Penny's gift of purposing to have more godly music in our home the next year. One of my sons gave the gift to Christ to make a greater investment in his younger brothers. Another son gave the gift of doing his part to have less strife with his siblings.

Yet another gave the gift of deciding to stand alone at school in order to preserve his witness for Christ. I write down all our gifts and rehearse them the next year at the special dinner for Christ that we discussed in an earlier chapter.

Being a vessel of love during any holiday celebration can certainly take a lot of different forms. It may be a note of encouragement to one who has invested in your life. It could be the gift of your presence in taking time to listen to an older person or taking one to lunch or dinner. Perhaps you could bake something, and you and your children deliver homemade packages to your neighbors, teachers, or to a community servant like a fireman or policeman. It may even involve inviting someone to be a part of your holiday celebration who otherwise would be alone. When Christ is the honored guest of your holiday celebrations, His love will flow to you and through you. It does not have to be a fanfare and will probably go unnoticed by many. However, if He prompts it and empowers it, it will be remembered and rewarded forever.

NOTE

1. This story is found under "The White Envelope" or "White Envelopes" and is readily available on the Internet. It was written by Nancy Gavin, and first published in *Woman's Day* magazine in 1982.

Chapter Seventeen

# Not Forgetting the "D" Word during the Holidays

A holiday season is often a more unstructured time, and this can be certainly welcomed and celebrated. However, I have discovered that if I neglect all aspects of personal discipline my spiritual, emotional, and physical well-being suffers. It results in neither a holy nor a happy holiday.

One needs to understand God's grace in order to cooperate with God's Spirit in leading a disciplined life. "Self-control" and discipline are a *fruit* of the Spirit's control and not human effort alone (Galatians 5:22–23)! However, it is clear that there is to be a human response to the Spirit in order to keep our lives under His control (cf. 1 Corinthians 9:24–27).

## FIND IT IN PROVERBS

The book of Proverbs is a valuable tool to aid one in gaining God's wisdom to live a disciplined and diligent life. I have often assigned students to study the topic of diligence in Proverbs. We can also learn about diligence by examining its contrast, slothfulness.

For many years I have read one chapter of Proverbs a day to correspond with the day of the month. For example, on the first of the month I read Proverbs 1 and on the second day of the month Proverbs 2 and so forth. Each month you can make it through the book. After doing this for many years I started gathering verses to trace topics. I have one topic in mind as I read Proverbs for that month. As I read my one chapter I would reference the verses that contributed to that topic. With hardly any extra effort, at the end of the month I had noted every verse that related to that topic. You could do that with the topic of diligence in Proverbs and engage in a life-changing study.

Holidays can be enjoyable times of celebrating and even feasting. There can be great joy in this, but when any blessing and even legitimate gift of God begins to control us—true joy will be lost.

All things are lawful for me, but not all things are profitable. All things are lawful for me, but I will not be mastered by anything. (1 Corinthians 6:12)

There is no doubt a fine line between keenly enjoying something and it beginning to control you. When we are being *ruled* by our desires and drives, we are in bondage and great spiritual danger. Ancient cities were protected by surrounding walls to guard them from an enemy invasion. With this background in mind we are able to understand Proverbs 25:28.

A person without self-control is like a city with broken-down walls. (NLT)

There is wisdom in maintaining a measure of discipline in your life in the midst of your holiday celebrations. It took some years to realize that this made for a better and more enjoyable holiday. Even in an especially unstructured day I discovered the wisdom of building my schedule around a few simple disciplines. A little exercise can keep you more alert to the Lord and the opportunities of the day. You may also discover that a walk around the block is what your body is craving even more than the third dessert!

*Even times of leisure need to be times of making wise choices.*

Even times of leisure need to be times of making wise choices. The Bible calls these wise choices approving "the things that are excellent" (Philippians 1:10). "Approving" refers to choosing or putting your stamp of approval on the very best ways to aid you in a life of love. A little forethought is often needed to make that type of choice. For some, it is choosing worthwhile reading materials. For others, it might mean planning times of group interactive games for your gatherings that make all feel included.

To be sure, there are times that your body, mind, and spirit need rest and a break from the routine. Even in this time it is wise to be sensitive to the Spirit and His loving desire to give you self-control. Keeping a measure of discipline in your life can often aid your joy in the Christmas holidays.

## PENNY'S Thoughts

The discipline of prayer and planning ahead is key for me to spiritually, emotionally, and physically enjoy any holiday. There have been one too many times when a celebration has left me absolutely drained and dreading the next time! Clearly I wasn't serving by the grace God supplies. Now, about a month before a major holiday, I'll review notes I've made from last year's celebration—these might include menus, shopping list of favors and special gifts, decorations, guest lists, seating arrangements, special activities, what worked, what didn't. Those notes have been a tremendous help to break the project down to manageable pieces. Most important, Bill and I lay the holiday before the Lord, asking Him what He wants to accomplish in that occasion. It is thrilling to see how He puts the guests, menu, and activities together to create a stimulating and uplifting time. Yes, I might come away tired, but so very blessed, and my love for God and others strengthened.

Chapter
Eighteen

# Preparing for *Temptation during the Holidays*

Holiday times can be a time of special temptation. We have alluded to this in chapter 1 when we looked at the spiritual pressures of the holidays. It is wise to foresee these spiritual dangers and prepare ourselves for them.

> A prudent person foresees danger and takes precautions. The simpleton goes on blindly and suffers the consequences. (Proverbs 22:3 NLT)

Some of the temptations can result from the lack of discipline during holidays. Even as committed Christians we can find ourselves wasting time or even defiling ourselves with media. As a student preparing for the ministry I could come home for a month during Christmas break and be tempted in my exhausted state to forget what life was all about. After working hard and finishing college, I enrolled in a rigorous graduate seminary program. I would come home and see friends who had entered the work field living comfortable lives. I would be tempted to ask myself, "Lord, am I missing it?" Even our minds need to be disciplined to reject the constant pull of our culture which defines one's purpose for living in a self-centered way.

Temptation begins in the realm of our thoughts, which lead to sinful words, actions, and habits. The point is that they begin with wrong thinking, and Jesus shed His blood to not only forgive us but also to liberate us to reject falsehood and replace it with truth. Present your mind and imagination to God as instruments for God to use for His righteous purpose (Romans 6:12–13). Ask God to

*Does the celebration of any part of your holiday make you feel less than special and delighted in by God as His child?*

aid you in discerning any wrong thoughts as you celebrate your holiday and obey the first prompting of the Spirit to reject the temptation to dwell on the lie.

Does the celebration of any part of your holiday make you feel less than special and delighted in by God as His child? Perhaps you are not paired up with someone on a special day like New Year's Eve or Christmas, and you begin to feel like you've been left out. If you have trusted Jesus Christ, you can delight in being one of God's chosen ones. Consider this little story:[1]

I grew up knowing I was different, and I hated it. I was born with a cleft palate, and when I started school, my classmates made it clear to me how I looked to others: a little girl with a misshapen lip, crooked nose, lopsided teeth, and garbled speech.

When schoolmates asked: What happened to your lip? I'd tell them I'd fallen and cut it on a piece of glass. Somehow it seemed more acceptable to have suffered an accident than to have been born different. I was convinced that no one outside my family could love me.

There was, however, a teacher in the second grade whom we all adored—Mrs. Leonard by name. She was short, round, happy—a sparkling lady.

Annually we had a hearing test . . . Mrs. Leonard gave the test to everyone in the class, and finally it was my turn. I knew from past years that we stood against the door and covered one ear, and the teacher sitting at her desk would whisper something, and we would have to repeat it back—things like "The sky is blue" or "Do you have new shoes?" I waited for those words that God must have put into her mouth, those seven words that changed my life.

Mrs. Leonard said, in her whisper, "I wish you were my little girl."

Let your battle in your thinking motivate you to rebuild your thought pattern with God's truth.[2] As you trust God to rest and refresh you, be sure to discern the difference between true rest and fleshy idleness that can be the opportunity for a spiritual decline. It is wise to know of your own vulnerabilities and to be on guard. A wise principle is found in Romans 13:14:

> But put on the Lord Jesus Christ, and make no provision for the flesh in regard to its lusts.

Perhaps you know of things that have tripped you up in holiday times in the past. Many have told me of their temptation to enter into a wrong relationship during this time. This can easily happen when a single person loses sight of God's values. During one holiday season I went through the Bible to note the things that God esteems in a woman. The purpose for this study in my singleness was to guide my mind, emotions, and will to be attracted to the right things. By putting some forethought in your battle, you can also request specific prayer support.

When you know that you are fully accepted by God, you can talk to God with complete honesty. This is what enables one to be intimate with Him. It is His perfect love that overcomes the fear of rejection (1 John 4:18). Why not come now with freedom to His throne of grace and receive His mercy and grace (Hebrews 4:15–16)?

Whatever struggle you may have, Jesus desires to speak a word of hope. He shed His blood not only to forgive you but also to liberate you. You are not stuck in any wrong pattern. As you submit completely to Him, resist the devil's message of despair and ask God to fill you with hope in your spirit for this holiday celebration.

NOTE

1. Mary Ann Bird tells this story in her memoir *The Whisper Test*. It has been recounted in numerous venues.
2. See pages 162–167 in my book *Living the Life God Has Planned* (Moody, 2001) for further help.

# PRACTICAL Help 14

## Other Ideas for Your Christmas Celebration

- One family plans a "spiritual gift" for their neighborhood. One year, it was a candy cane with a Bible verse. Another year, it was a Christmas craft that the children made with a letter from their family that contained a Christian witness. It was the children's job to pull their red wagon from house to house and deliver the gifts.

- One year, this family set up a prayer mailbox on their covered porch. They sent a note to their neighbors expressing their love and care for them. In it, they told them about the prayer mailbox. If someone was hurting or needed prayer, they could put their request in the box—anonymously if they wished—and the family would be sure to pray for them.

- Penny's mother has a video recording of Handel's *Messiah*. Every Christmas since the children were young, she would have that playing in the background while the children were enjoying their new toys on the floor. They were very interested and amused by the orchestra and the soloists.

- We have a treasured illustrated book of the Luke 2 Christmas story. Many mornings during the advent season, Penny would snuggle on the couch with the children and read this story over and over. With repetition, they were able to "read" some of the pages with Penny and thus commit that wonderful passage to memory.

- Our church encourages children to have Christmas cocoa parties, inviting friends and neighbors to enjoy Christmas goodies while singing Christmas carols and hearing the Luke 2 account of Christ's birth. You can host it after school, sending invitations in advance so the special day can be set aside.

- Sing Christmas carols to your neighbors and friends.

- Read the Christmas story out loud with different family members taking a part or role.

- Turn off the television and go on a long walk as a family, praying for your neighborhood.
- Drive an elderly neighbor or friend around to see decorated homes.
- Offer a single mom or dad a day off and take their children on an adventure to a sporting event, park, or zoo.
- Escort a widow or widower to a Christian movie or play.

Some of the ideas were inspired by articles in *Focus on the Family* December 2008 and an article in a December 2007 publication of Crown Financial Ministries (visit crown.org).

# Section Six
*Other Holidays*

Chapter
Nineteen

Martin Luther
King Day:
*Let Justice
Roll Down
Like Waters*

## "I HAVE A DREAM"

Most of us recognize the speaker of this short phrase. It is Martin Luther King Jr. the great civil rights leader.

Most of us have dreams, but on this holiday it is meaningful to examine Dr. King's dreams and see how our nation has changed since he made his famous speech in 1963, examine where we still need to improve, and determine how we as Christians can observe his legacy with purpose.

## THE BACKGROUND
## OF DR. KING'S MINISTRY

The America we know today is a different place from the America of Dr. King's time, thanks largely in part to this Baptist minister's efforts and sacrifices. At one time, our nation had separate drinking fountains for whites and for people of color—not only that, but separate swimming places, restaurants, public schools, transportation, and so on. These norms were mandated by Jim Crow laws—state and local laws that created "separate but equal" status for black Americans. The idea was that all Americans would be given the same opportunities but that the races were better kept separate.

When Thomas Jefferson wrote the Declaration of Independence, he stated, "all men are created equal." He meant that everyone should have the chance to work hard and make their dreams come true. The reality under the Jim Crow laws, however, was an institutional system that led to unequal treatment and inferior accommodations for nonwhite people, which in turn led to disadvantages in educational, economic, and other opportunities.

## EVERYDAY LIFE

It might be difficult today to understand the cultural system Dr. King wanted to change. Let's look at a couple of aspects of ordinary life we might take for granted.

Imagine going to school in a dilapidated building, being taught by teachers who were poorly paid and not well prepared, having inadequate transportation to get there, and being offered very little in sports or other extracurricular activities. Now imagine that you need to travel quite a distance to get to this school, but that there is a very good school closer to where you live.

Today we might think, *Just go to the school closer to your home. That makes sense.* But back in the fifties, the schools were segregated. That means that even though a school was near your home, if it was a whites-only facility and you were not white, you were not allowed to enroll there.

Some visionary and brave people challenged this system, and the Supreme Court decided in the 1954 case *Brown vs. the Board of Education of Topeka* that state laws that established separate public schools for different races and thus denied black children the opportunity for equal educational opportunities were unconstitutional. You can read about this on the Internet and through other sources.

Now picture yourself going to a restaurant or out for fast food and being told you could not be served because you were not white. What would you do?

In 1960, four young men entered a Woolworth store in Greensboro, North Carolina, and sat down at the lunch counter. These men were black, and the diner had a strict policy of serving whites only. One of the men, Franklin McCain, describes how he felt when he decided to enter the eating establishment like anyone else, rather than be afraid to do so: "I had the most wonderful feeling. I had a feeling of liberation, restored manhood."[1]

The men noticed an older white woman sitting at the counter a few stools away, and assumed they knew what she was thinking: *These men don't belong here. I wish they'd leave.* But she surprised them. She said, "Boys, I am so proud of you. I only regret that you didn't do this ten years ago." McCain said later, "What I learned from that little incident was . . . don't you ever, ever stereotype anybody in this life until you at least experience them and have the opportunity to talk to them. . . . I'm always open to people who speak differently, who look differently, and who come from different places."[2]

That day, the four men stayed at the lunch counter until the store closed. The next day they came back with fifteen friends, the next three hundred; and eventually a thousand people participated in this peaceful type of protest called a sit-in.

## NEW LAWS

When President Lyndon B. Johnson signed the Civil Rights Act of 1964, Martin Luther King Jr. was among the guests standing near him. This law forbade discrimination in employment, and provided for the integration of schools and other public places.

A good way to remember Dr. King's work and influence is to read about his life and learn about the cultural norms that he knew must be changed. He and his family made many sacrifices to change unjust systems in society, not only for the people of his time, but also for generations to come. You'll want to read about the March on Washington for Jobs and Freedom on August 28, 1963, when he gave his famous "I Have a Dream" speech from the steps of the Lincoln Memorial.

*Martin and his family made many sacrifices, not only for the people of his time, but also for generations to come.*

Excerpts from this speech are reprinted on page 173. If Dr. King were giving a speech today, do you think he would change any of these words?

## ATTITUDES

Even though laws were now enacted that prohibited legal discrimination, the hearts and minds of individuals take longer to change. Earlier in 1963, Dr. King and his staff led nonviolent protests in Birmingham, Alabama, and were greeting with angry officials who set police dogs on them, sprayed them with water cannons, and hit them with sticks. Men, women, teenagers, and children were part of the crowd that were recipients of this treatment.

When Dr. King gave his speech in Washington, he referred to these events and others like them and said, "In the process of gaining our rightful place, we must not be guilty of wrong deeds. Let us not seek to satisfy our thirst for freedom by drinking from the cup of bitterness and hatred." How does this admonition compare with Jesus' words in Matthew 5:38–40? Also read Matthew 5:1–16.

## WHAT DOES GOD SAY?

There is a thirst in every heart to feel like you belong, to feel you have value, and to be fully accepted. These thirsts can only be fully satisfied in Jesus. (See John 7:37–39.) The term *Imago Dei*—image of God—expresses the truth that because mankind has been made in God's image, each person has inherent dignity and worth. This is true even for fallen man. (See Genesis 9:6; James 3:9.) The image of God has been marred by sin but not erased. It is due to the fall or the coming of sin in the world that there has been the exploitation and injustice of various groups throughout human history.

Individuals who have placed their trust in Christ are new creatures (2 Corinthians 5:17), and are being conformed to His image (Romans 8:29; 2 Corinthians 3:18). Part of this involves caring for the poor and those with special needs (James 1:27), and honoring and doing good to all (Galatians 6:10; 1 Peter 2:17). The command to "honor all" in 1 Peter 2:17 is a great verse to meditate on for this holiday. What else does God ask us to do? Think and talk about in what other ways we can be instrumental in following what Jesus Himself has prayed for the world: "[May] your kingdom come. Your will be done, on earth as it is in heaven." God's will is already being done in heaven; what is our part in having God's will be done on earth?

## DREAMING

Perhaps the most famous part of Dr. King's speech is the following:

> I say to you today, my friends, even though we face the difficulties of today and tomorrow, I still have a dream. It is a dream deeply rooted in the American dream. . . . I have a dream that one day this nation will rise up and live out the true meaning of its creed: "We hold these truths to be self-evident: that all men are created equal." . . . I have a dream that my four little children will one day live in a nation where they will not be judged by the color of their skin but by the content of their character.

Sadly, Martin Luther King Jr.'s life was cut short by an assassin's bullet in Memphis on April 4, 1968. Do you think his dreams have been realized in our nation? In what ways? In what ways have they not?

## NEIGHBORS

What is your neighborhood like? Is it made up mostly of people who are about the same in race, ethnicity, income, and education level? Are most of the people you know white collar or blue collar? How can you meet and get to know people who are different than you are?

Perhaps you live in a more diverse area and are fortunate to know people with an assortment of backgrounds. What is interesting about knowing a variety of people? What do you have in common with people of a different race than you?

Someone has said that the most segregated hour in America is eleven o'clock on Sunday morning. It is true that many of our churches are homogenous, that is, made up mostly of one type of people rather than of a diversity of backgrounds. The reasons for this are many, and are beyond the scope of our purpose here, but it is worth reflecting on as we seek to honor Martin Luther King Jr. and his legacy. How is the lack of diversity in our churches a heart matter? What do we do when our neighborhood or suburb changes racially or ethnically? How do we as Christians deal with "white flight" or other such negative reactions?

*God's will is already being done in heaven; what is our part in having God's will be done on earth?*

There are countless ways we can keep Dr. King's legacy alive—from learning about the civil rights movement that he sparked, to reaching out to those who are different from us in our own neighborhoods. But perhaps the most important way is to apply heart and hand to bring to fruition what Jesus prayed for His followers, and for each of us: "That they may all be one; even as You, Father, are in Me and I in You, that they also may be in Us, so that the world may believe that You sent me" (John 17:21). "And he has given us this command: Those who love God must also love one another" (1 John 4:21).

NOTES

1. http://www.npr.org/templates/story/story.php?storyId=18615556.
2. Ibid.

# PRACTICAL Help 15
## "I Have a Dream" speech (excerpts), given August 28, 1963 on the steps of the Lincoln Memorial in Washington, D.C.

I am happy to join with you today in what will go down in history as the greatest demonstration for freedom in the history of our nation.

Five score years ago, a great American, in whose symbolic shadow we stand today, signed the Emancipation Proclamation. This momentous decree came as a great beacon light of hope to millions of Negro slaves who had been seared in the flames of withering injustice. It came as a joyous daybreak to end the long night of their captivity.

But one hundred years later, the Negro still is not free. One hundred years later, the life of the Negro is still sadly crippled by the manacles of segregation and the chains of discrimination. One hundred years later, the Negro lives on a lonely island of poverty in the midst of a vast ocean of material prosperity. One hundred years later, the Negro is still languishing in the corners of American society and finds himself an exile in his own land. So we have come here today to dramatize a shameful condition.

In a sense we have come to our nation's capital to cash a check. When the architects of our republic wrote the magnificent words of the Constitution and the Declaration of Independence, they were signing a promissory note to which every American was to fall heir. This note was a promise that all men, yes, black men as well as white men, would be guaranteed the unalienable rights of life, liberty, and the pursuit of happiness.

We must forever conduct our struggle on the high plane of dignity and discipline. We must not allow our creative protest to degenerate into physical violence. Again and again we must rise to the majestic heights of meeting physical force with soul force. The marvelous new militancy which has engulfed the Negro community must not lead us to a distrust of all white people, for many of our white brothers, as evidenced by their presence here today, have come to realize that their destiny is tied up with our destiny. They have come to realize that their freedom is inextricably bound to our freedom. We cannot walk alone.

I say to you today, my friends, so even though we face the difficulties of today and tomorrow, I still have a dream. It is a dream deeply rooted in the American dream.

I have a dream that one day this nation will rise up and live out the true meaning of its creed: "We hold these truths to be self-evident: that all men are created equal."

This is our hope. This is the faith that I go back to the South with. With this faith we will be able to hew out of the mountain of despair a stone of hope. With this faith we will be able to transform the jangling discords of our nation into a beautiful symphony of brotherhood. With this faith we will be able to work together, to pray together, to struggle together, to go to jail together, to stand up for freedom together, knowing that we will be free one day.

This will be the day when all of God's children will be able to sing with a new meaning, "My country, 'tis of thee, sweet land of liberty, of thee I sing. Land where my fathers died, land of the pilgrim's pride, from every mountainside, let freedom ring."

And if America is to be a great nation this must become true. So let freedom ring from the prodigious hilltops of New Hampshire. Let freedom ring from the mighty mountains of New York. Let freedom ring from the heightening Alleghenies of Pennsylvania!

Let freedom ring from the snowcapped Rockies of Colorado!

Let freedom ring from the curvaceous slopes of California!

But not only that; let freedom ring from Stone Mountain of Georgia!

Let freedom ring from Lookout Mountain of Tennessee!
Let freedom ring from every hill and molehill of Mississippi.
From every mountainside, let freedom ring.

And when this happens, when we allow freedom to ring, when we let it ring from every village and every hamlet, from every state and every city, we will be able to speed up that day when all of God's children, black men and white men, Jews and Gentiles, Protestants and Catholics, will be able to join hands and sing in the words of the old Negro spiritual, "Free at last! free at last! thank God Almighty, we are free at last!"

# PRACTICAL Help 16
## Other suggestions for a Martin Luther King Day Celebration:

- Watch a video of Dr. King delivering his famous "I Have a Dream" speech. You can find one on YouTube.com.

- Share some of the injustices and hurts people experience in our nation because of racism. What might God be asking you to do about these?

- Visit a church in a different neighborhood or a church that has a different racial or ethnic makeup than yours.

- If you live in or visit the Chicago area, go to the DuSable Museum of African American History. If you cannot go, check out the museum's website: www.dusablemuseum.org.

- Go to the public library and find books about accomplished African American citizens: George Washington Carver, Frederick Douglass, Jackie Robinson, Marian Anderson, Condoleezza Rice, and others. Find out when they lived and how their lives were influential.

- With younger children: Make paper chains with black, red, white, yellow, brown construction paper representing different skin tones found in our country. Tell the children that each link represents a hand, and Dr. King wanted all people in our nation to join hands. A variation on this activity would be for children to trace their hands onto different colored paper.

- Make up a quiz about Dr. King:

1. Where and when was he born?
2. Where and when did he die?
3. What was his wife's name?
4. How many children did he have?
5. He won the Nobel Peace Prize in 1964. What distinguished him from other recipients of this prize?
6. Name some of the books he wrote.
7. What was Dr. King's profession?
8. What was significant about Montgomery, Alabama, in the civil rights movement?
9. When Martin was in grade school, what song did his teacher have the class sing every morning?
10. What foreign figure influenced Dr. King in nonviolent resistance?

## Answers

1. Atlanta, Georgia; January 15, 1929
2. Memphis, Tennessee; April 4, 1968
3. Coretta Scott King
4. Four
5. At the age of thirty-five, he was the youngest to have won it up to that time.
6. *Stride Toward Freedom: The Montgomery Story; Strength to Love; Why We Can't Wait; Where Do We Go from Here: Chaos or Community?*
7. He was a minister; in 1954 he became pastor of the Dexter Avenue Baptist Church in Montgomery, Alabama.

8. Dr. King led the black boycott of the city's buses because of their policy of segregation.
9. "Lift Every Voice and Sing"
10. Mahatma Ghandi of India

For further reading: *The Humanitarian Jesus* by Christian Buckley and Ryan Dobson (Moody, 2010).

Chapter
Twenty

Valentine's Day:
*An Opportunity
to Experience
Christ's Love*

On February 14 thousands of people celebrate Valentine's Day—a celebration of love and lovers. Its history is traced to paying honor to the Roman god of fertility at the Feast of Lupercalia, which even then was celebrated on February 14. It is still seen as a day to "fall in love." Since February 14 was formerly thought to be the first day that birds mated, this sparked the custom of sending Valentines.

Valentine's Day does provide an opportunity to celebrate. Over one billion dollars are spent on chocolate alone around this holiday.[1] During the rest of the year women are responsible for 75 percent of chocolate purchases. However, men buy 75 percent of the chocolate consumed around this holiday.[2]

## OUR NEED FOR LOVE

What should we as Christians keep in mind when this holiday comes around year after year? We must realize that the most fundamental need that God has placed in our hearts is the need to be loved. This need is not something that will ever go away. This need for love can draw people into immorality and wrong choices as they seek to meet this need in unrighteous ways. A Christian has learned to take this "thirst" for love to Jesus, who said, "If anyone is thirsty, let him come to Me and drink" (John 7:37).

## OUR NEED FOR A PERFECT LOVER

One of the ways that the Bible describes a believer's relationship with Christ is in terms of a marriage to Christ (see Romans 7:1–6). One cannot fully appreciate the wonder of Christ's love without first understanding their prior predicament.

If you carefully examine this passage you will observe that becoming a Christian involves a transition from being married to the law to now being married to Christ. God's love is a holy love, and we have violated His holy law. Our former marriage partner—the law—makes righteous demands but the result is only a sense of condemnation because of our failure to meet these demands.

How would you like to be in a relationship with someone who only put expectations on you, gave you no help or encouragement to meet these expectations, and condemned you every time you failed? The trouble with our situation was not the law, which is holy, righteous, and good (verse12), but rather our rebellious nature. Jesus came to earth and set His love upon us in our ungodly, helpless, and sinful state (Romans 5:8). Only when we realize our condemnation and our hopeless desire to perform for love, can we begin to rest in and enjoy our relationship with a Perfect Lover.

## THE DYNAMICS OF A MARRIAGE OF CHRIST

We needed a marriage partner who could do more than just give us perfect advice. The law could do that, but we stood condemned in our unwillingness and inability to keep its good counsel. Marriage involves mutual sharing of resources, and our infinitely rich Spouse shares with us everything we need to fellowship with Him ("life") and to reflect Him ("godliness").

Seeing that His divine power has granted to us everything pertaining to life and godliness, through the true knowledge of Him who called us by His own glory and excellence. (2 Peter 1:3)

In Christ we have every spiritual blessing because in Him we have everything we need to fulfill His will for us.

Blessed be the God and Father of our Lord Jesus Christ, who has blessed us with every spiritual blessing in the heavenly places in Christ. (Ephesians 1:3)

So then let no one boast in men. For all things belong to you, whether Paul or Apollos or Cephas or the world or life or death or things present or things to come; *all things* belong to you, and you belong to Christ; and Christ belongs to God. (1 Corinthians 3:21–23)

Valentine's Day is a time to celebrate His great love for us in His providing for us. It is a day to be content as we realize and enjoy His loving provisions. Ask Him to open your eyes to realize how rich you are. This is the prayer of Ephesians 1:15–23. Make it your prayer this Valentine's Day.

## REPLACING STRONGHOLDS WITH GOD'S LIBERATING TRUTH

A "stronghold" is a term used to describe a thought pattern that gives Satan a protected place of influence. We need to trust God to uproot any lie that is not consistent with God's liberating truth that is revealed in the Bible. Valentine's Day is a time to celebrate His amazing love for us. He who knows everything we have ever thought, said, and done—delights in us. He does not merely pity us but delights in us as an artist delights in his masterpiece.

On this holiday especially we can embrace the truth that a Christian is beloved of God and treasured by Him—which is why we are called His inheritance (Psalm 94:14). One who is treasured by God must identify and resist the wicked lies of such thoughts as "No one could possibly love me," "I'm no good," or "I'll never amount to anything." Recognize that one's emotional interpretation of certain life experiences may make them feel less then cherished and loved. Thoughts such as "I didn't get picked," "I'm unattractive," or "I've been left on the shelf" are strongholds that need to be replaced with God's truth.

Test your thoughts by the following chart.

| What I feel or think about myself | What God says about me as a Christian according to Scripture |
|---|---|
| I am unworthy and unacceptable. | I accept you. Romans 15:7 |
| I am alone. | I'll live in you and you'll never have to be alone as I had to be when I died on the cross for you. (Galatians 2:20; Hebrews 13:5–6) |
| I am not special to anyone or loved. | You are a precious person to Me, and I am continually thinking about you. (Psalm 139:17–18) |
| I do not have what it takes to be successful in life. | I'm continually devoted to you and will provide all your need to fulfill My purpose for you. (Romans 8:31–32, 38–39) |
| I feel totally responsible for my life. | I've adopted you into My family and will take care of you, lead you, discipline you, and develop you as My child. (Galatians 4:5–6; Romans 8:14) |
| I feel despair as I think of the future. | I have a wonderful future for you that you will know joy and satisfaction for all eternity. (Romans 8:18) |
| I fear Satan's power over my life. | I have defeated Satan, and as you submit to My loving authority, you can experience freedom. (James 4:7; I John 4:4) |
| I cannot overcome my sin habits. | I sent My Son to liberate you from sin's power, and you are a winner and can now live in His strength. (Romans 6:11–13) |
| I have no direction or plan for my life. | I have a unique plan of good works for you to accomplish. (Ephesians 2:10) |
| I am not as qualified to fulfill God's plan as other people that I know. | My plan is unique for you because no one else has your exact physical features, upbringing, talents and abilities, and even your unique weaknesses. (Psalm 139:13–16) |

| What I feel or think about myself | What God says about me as a Christian according to Scripture |
|---|---|
| I don't think I can keep on going. | I'll continue to work in you because My glory is at stake. (Philippians 2:13; Psalm 22:3) |
| I am not attractive and fear failure. | I'll make you into a most attractive person in My eyes and allow you to fulfill My plan as you present your life to Me. (Romans 8:29; 12:1–2) |

Thoughts lead to actions, and actions to habits. It is these lies that contribute to eight thousand teenagers a day being affected by sexually transmitted diseases, and one million a year becoming pregnant out of wedlock. February 14 was also declared a Day of Purity by Governor Taft of Ohio and is celebrated by people across our nation by renewing their commitment to stay sexually pure in mind and actions. This stems from the desire to be respected for who they are and not as an object of lust to be discarded after it is used. It stems from the desire to yield all that we are to God and our sexual energies to Him and our spouse in His timing and will.

If we are under God's loving command to "have no other gods before Me" (Exodus 20:3), why not use this as a basis for a prayer of faith? Ask the Lord to uproot any ideas in your mind that are not true and worthy of Him. Believe Him to enable you to recognize these lies in a way that they can be rejected and replaced with His liberating truth. The following is a prayer that I have shared with thousands of people. While there is nothing magic about the words, each concept in the prayer is something for which we can all believe God.

*"God, I want to know You above all else in life. I need the motivation, encouragement, and the wisdom to know how; but I desire it*

*and want to desire it more. I believe You will overcome all obstacles
and accomplish this in my life!*

*For Your name's sake and for my eternal benefit. Amen."*

### HAPPY VALENTINE'S DAY!!!

## PENNY'S Thoughts

Valentine's Day has never been a major celebration in our
family . . . maybe because I have three sons! Yes, I would bake
something special and give them a Valentine love note, explaining the qualities I so appreciate in them. We would also make
Valentines to send to our elderly friends and relatives. But recently
I became excited about using this day to promote biblical agape
love. Below are some thoughts.

- Read and discuss St. Valentine's story. This story was taken
  from David Rigg's sermon, which can be found at
  http://www.sermoncentral.com/sermons/how-
  christians-should-celebrate-valentines-day-david-rigg-
  sermon-on-christian-love-118198.asp?page=1.

Around 250 years after Jesus was born, there was a priest by the
name of Valentine living in Rome at the time that Claudius was the
emperor of Rome. He was known as Claudius the Cruel. Claudius
wanted a big army and believed that men should volunteer to join.
However, many men had no desire to leave home and go off to
battle. Consequently, not many of them signed up for the Roman
army. Claudius thought that at the root of this disinterest was the
men's desire to stay with their wives and children. Emperor Claudius
was livid with anger. He thought, "What if men were not married?
Wouldn't they be more inclined to join my army?" So Claudius
decreed that there would be no more marriages. Young people
thought his new law was cruel; Valentine thought it was unbiblical.
One of his favorite duties as a priest was to marry people. After

Emperor Claudius passed his law, Valentine continued to perform marriage ceremonies—but in secret. He would whisper the words of the marriage ceremony, while listening for soldiers on the steps outside.

One night, those footsteps came. The couple he was marrying fled, but he was caught by Claudius's soldiers and thrown in jail. His punishment? Death. While in prison, Valentine tried to remain cheerful. Many young people came to visit him, throwing flowers and notes up to his window. They wanted him to know that they were grateful for his stance on the issue of marriage.

One of these young people was the daughter of the prison guard. Her father allowed her to visit him in his cell. They often sat and talked for hours. She believed he did the right thing by ignoring the emperor's edict and performing marriage ceremonies. On the day Valentine died, he left her a note thanking her for her friendship and loyalty. He signed it, "Love from your Valentine." That note started the custom of exchanging love notes on Valentine's Day. It was written on the day he died, February 14, 269.

Thoughts for discussion:

*When is it right to resist the governing authorities?*

*How did Valentine stand up for biblical truths?*

*Read John 15:13. How did Valentine illustrate this verse? What other ways, besides literal death, are we to die to ourselves?*

*What one way could you sacrifice your wants for the needs of others in your family, at church, in the neighborhood, on your team, at school, and with friends?*

- Invite a group of young students to your home for an edifying evening on loving God and others. One year David, our

youngest, suggested that we have our Spanish class over. He
and I were having a wonderful time taking the class
together. The students' ages ranged from sixth grade to college . . . and then there was me. Our class of ten plus our
teacher came for a Mexican Mountain dinner. Each student
brought an ingredient to contribute.

After dinner, we played games in Spanish and then sat
down to watch *The Moment After: The Beginning of the End*
in Spanish with English subtitles. (This movie can be found
at christiancinema.com.)

This movie is about the end times and wonderfully
illustrates the passionate love for the Lord and the "dying to
self" love for others that should characterize our lives as
Christians. In closing, we prayed that our lives would be
filled with grace to love in such a way. After everyone had
gone home for the evening, David asked, "Can we do the
same thing next year?" *Mmm*, I thought, *there is a sequel to
this movie.* "Sounds like a great idea, honey!"

This activity can of course be done at any time of year,
but Valentine's Day gave us a chance to spark a discussion
of loving God and others.

• Have an annual "State of the Union" private dinner or week-
end with your spouse. Valentine's Day might be a great
reminder to do this if your anniversary falls at a busier time
of year. You might consider rereading your marriage vows,
praying for each other in the concerns each carries, sharing
what you appreciate in the other, recalling special memories
of the past year, or reading 1 Corinthians 13 as a base for
discussion about one way the Lord might desire for you to
grow in love.

• Invite someone for dinner to tell your family how they
share the love of Christ where God has placed them: a missionary, foster parents, someone who tutors students in
public school, or someone who volunteers in a nursing

home. Including some ordinary people (as well as those in Christian "professions") will affirm them and also show kids that God uses people in many ways. You might include some of the older members of your church who do not often get out, or some new people who are just beginning to visit your church. Be sure to find out how you can pray for your guests and if possible, do it before the guests leave.

- Read Matthew 25:31–40. Visit a nursing home or work together as a family, ministering to the homeless or refugees or whatever needs God highlights for you and your family.

The Lord allowed us to pick up a sixth grade Burmese refugee for "Upward" Basketball, a Christian sports ministry at our church. What a blessing it has been for my son and our family to see this dear one blossom these past two years!

There are many opportunities to show love, and God will show you what is right at a given time.

NOTES
1. holidayinsights.com.
2. Ibid.

Chapter
Twenty-One

Presidents' Day:
*Honoring a
Sovereign God*

In 1971 a law enacted by Congress created a federal holiday to be known as Presidents' Day. It is observed on the third Monday of February in honor of all the past presidents of our country. Prior to 1971, the February 22 birthday of George Washington and the February 12 birthday of Abraham Lincoln were observed as national holidays in most states. How does a Christian in this country or in any country celebrate a holiday that is in honor of the president of his country?

## UNDERSTAND A CHRISTIAN'S
## VIEW OF HISTORY

Is history a series of meaningless events? If we believe it is, we can become frustrated and even despairing. If we do not understand who we are, where we've been, and where we're headed, life is merely an attempt to find happiness in the present.

A believer has a relationship with the One who is exalted as head "over all" and rules "over all" (1 Chronicles 29:11–12). We also read that the "pillars of the earth are the Lord's, and He set the world on them" (1 Samuel 2:8).

In the midst of great pressure and opposition, Hezekiah declared that God alone was the God "of all the kingdoms of the earth" (2 Kings 19:15). In the midst of his pain Job confessed the truth that in God's hand is "the life of every living thing and the breath of all mankind" (Job 12:10). God is to be praised for His sovereign throne in the heavens and for the fact that His kingdom rules over all (Psalm 103:19). In any and every circumstance the believer has the assurance that His heavenly Father is working all things after the counsel of His will and for the ultimate good of His people (Ephesians 1:11; Romans 8:28–29).

## UNDERSTAND GOD'S
## SOVEREIGN RULE AND WILL

On Presidents' Day we can be glad that the sovereign God rules over all things.

God's rule can be seen in three ways. First of all, we see His eternal rule over creation (2 Chronicles 20:6; 1 Timothy 1:17). Secondly, God rules over His redeemed people as they submit to Him. In the case of Presidents Washington and Lincoln, both professed to trust Jesus Christ as their Savior. Washington's words on his tombstone are that he based his eternal hope "on the righteousness of Jesus Christ alone." Every true Christian has been transferred from the kingdom of darkness to the kingdom of Christ (Colossians 1:13). The third way that Scripture speaks of His rule is His future millennial and eternal kingdom when His judgment will fall on all who refuse to submit to His wise and loving rule (Revelation 20:1–22:21).

*Government does not always fulfill its divine purpose, but our sovereign God still accomplishes His providential will.*

God's will can also be viewed in three ways. It can refer to the prescriptive will or what He desires. For example, God is holy and does not desire sin; He also declares that it is His will for all people to be saved (1 Timothy 2:4). In His prescriptive will, God has righteous desires for all in authority. In His permissive will, God has allowed evil and permits people to reject Him. The sovereign God is never out of control, but each day He observes human authorities who do not fulfill His desires. In His providential will God overrules evil for good as evidenced by His using the greatest crime to become the world's greatest blessing (Matthew 21:42). God even used the unjust governing authorities in fulfilling His promises to bless the world through His precious Son, who was crucified at their hands.

## UNDERSTAND HOW TO VIEW
## GOVERNMENTAL AUTHORITY

Believers view all authority in light of their relationship to a sovereign God. All authority ultimately derives its authority from God and is there only by His permission. This truth is clearly taught throughout Scripture in such places as Psalms 75:6–7; Proverbs 21:1; Daniel 2:21; 4:17, 25, 32; 5:21; and Romans 13:1–7. Look at how Jesus affirmed this truth in John 19:11!

To say that God is sovereign over all authority is not to necessarily say that God is pleased with all rulers. In fact, the role of all in authority is to serve those under them. Our human nature tends to use those under our authority for our self-centered goals rather than to work for what is best for them.

God will judge all those in authority in regard to how they use their position. This is not only true of all governmental authority (Isaiah 24:21) but also of all employers who did not pay a fair wage (Malachi 3:5). Even a first-century master was reminded to treat his slave with consideration because he also had a Master in heaven to whom he was accountable (Colossians 4:1)!

First Peter 2:14 explains God's purpose for government—to reward and promote good and decent behavior and punish evil. It is to promote order and tranquil living (1 Timothy 2:1–2). Obviously government does not always fulfill its divine purpose, but our sovereign God still accomplishes His providential will.

## HOW TO RESPOND TO
## GOVERNMENTAL AUTHORITY

The Christian is given some clear instructions in regard to their response to government. The first of these is to submit to governing authority. This command to submit can be clearly seen in passages such as Romans 13:1; Titus 3:1; and 1 Peter 2:13–17.

Two reasons to submit to the government authorities can be found in Romans 13:1–7. One is that the sovereign God is the ultimate source of all authority, and He puts governments in place for our good (verse 4). Rebelling against government will lead to retribution and negative consequences. Of course the notable exception is if a government asks a believer to do something clearly against God's moral law. In this case the believer must graciously submit to God and be willing to suffer the consequences (cf. Acts 5:29; cf. 4:19–20).

The second reason to submit to government is to do it for the sake of his conscience (Romans 13:5). In other words, one is to submit to the government not only in the fear of the government who has the authority to enforce the law but also to submit in the fear of God. Such submission is to be an expression of one's personal relationship with God.

Believers are not only to submit to the government but also to pray for those in authority. Paul instructed Timothy as to what was the matter of first importance for the gathered church. When God's people come together, the matter of first importance according to 1 Timothy 2:1–2 is to pray and most notably for those in authority.

We have stated that government does not always fulfill God's perceptive will. It is God's wisdom that is needed in order for one to rule in a manner that fulfills His highest desires (Proverbs 8:15–16). We must remember that the heart of any authority is ultimately in the hands of our sovereign God (Proverbs 21:1). It is also true that the sovereign God has chosen to work through the prayers of His people. It is for this reason that it is to be declared to be of first importance in 1 Timothy 2:1–2.

What if every time we are tempted to speak ill of a government leader, we took it as encouragement to pray for him or her? We not only will enhance our relationship with God, but we would also have a more constructive influence on government.

## BELIEVER'S CELEBRATION OF PRESIDENTS' DAY

There is no better way to celebrate this holiday than to pray for the president of the United States and the government that he leads.

We can thank Him for godly men with whom He has graciously blessed our country in the past as this holiday is rooted in the celebration of George Washington and Abraham Lincoln. We can also ask God to remind His people to pray every time we are tempted to be critical of government. Such a response would be a fitting Christian response to this national holiday.

*There is no better way to celebrate this holiday than to pray for the president of the United States and the government that he leads.*

How might we pray? Let me offer a few examples of how God might lead you to pray. More important is for you to ask God to give you a prayer burden for the government. In so doing some of these requests may become a very part of the fabric of your heart that prompts you to respond to God's Spirit in prayer.

- Pray that your governing authority would fear God and recognize their accountability to Him (Proverbs 9:10).

- Pray that they would recognize their own inadequacy in a way that prompts them to seek God and His strength and wisdom (James 1:5).

- Pray that they would be given godly counsel and advisors who fear God (Proverbs 24:6).

- Pray for their marriage and family.

- Pray that they would desire purity and avoid pornography, perversion, and drunkenness.

- Pray that they would be honest in all their financial and ethical matters.

- Pray that they would have the courage to do right and be able to resist manipulation, bribery, and the fear of man.

- Pray that they would be shielded from the occult.

- Pray that they would be presented with biblical principles and promote the sanctity of life, the family, and morality.

- Pray that they would be prepared to give account to an almighty God.

Of course, you could add others to the above list. Sites such as http://ifapray.org (Intercessors for America) or http://presidentialprayerteam.com are valuable resources for current issues and timely reminders on how to pray for our country's leaders. In recent years I have by God's grace in some way sought to support the president in prayer each day. Presidents' Day is not merely a holiday for us as believers. It is also a time to renew our commitment to respond in prayerful submission to those in authority over us.

## PENNY'S Thoughts

While I was growing up, my mother would display two bronze plaques on the buffet during the month of February—one having the raised profile of George Washington and the other of Abraham Lincoln. During the course of one dinner, we discussed as a family the positive qualities of George Washington and ended the dinner with cherry pie. Another evening the discussion centered on Abraham Lincoln and ended with a chocolate rolled "Lincoln log" cake. These celebrations laid an important biblical groundwork for honoring those in authority.

In recent times my father would read his grandchildren the account of George Washington crossing the Delaware from the book *The Light and the Glory for Children* by Marshall, Manuel, and Fishel. They would then get on the floor with building blocks and Playmobiles and reenact that special night, which gloriously displays God's sovereignty in the affairs of men. My youngest son, David, might have been four or five years old at that time, but now at age twelve he can still recount the details, and most importantly he can see the hand of God at work for our young nation.

The following are other suggestions for your Presidents' Day celebration:

- Read aloud another wonderful book that highlights God's providential care: *The Bulletproof George Washington* by David Barton ISBN 0-925279-14-5. For a copy of this book, go to Amazon.com or write:

    WallBuilder Press
    P.O. Box 397
    Aledo, TX 76008
    817-441-6044

- Older Children would benefit from reading *The Making of George Washington* by William H. Wilbur or *Abraham Lincoln: The Man and His Faith* by G. Frederick Owen.
- Read *The Gettysburg Address by Abraham Lincoln* illustrated by Michael McCurdy (published by Houghton Mifflin Company). Repeated reading of this short book would greatly aid children in committing this important document to memory and understanding its meaning.
- George Washington had wonderful axioms[1] he wrote down and lived by. Try reading and discussing these as a family.

*Freedom:* Liberty, when it begins to take root, is a plant of rapid growth.

*Success:* When a man does all he can, though it succeeds not well, blame not him that did it.

*Marriage:* I have always considered marriage as the most interesting event of one's life, the foundation of happiness or misery.

*Conflict, Preparation:* To be prepared for war is one of the most effectual means of preserving peace.

*Friendship:* True friendship is a plant of slow growth, and must undergo and withstand the shocks of adversity before it is entitled to the appellation.

*Reputation:* Associate yourself with men of good quality if you esteem your own reputation; for 'tis better to be alone than in bad company.

*Conflict; Worry and Fear:* Worry is the interest paid by those who borrow trouble.

*Justice:* The best and only safe road to honor, glory, and true dignity is justice.

*Politics:* Government is not reason; it is not eloquent; it is force. Like fire, it is a dangerous servant and a fearful master.

NOTE
1. These quotes are found at www.jimpoz.com/quotes.

Chapter
Twenty-Two

# St. Patrick's Day:
## *Cultivating a Missionary Spirit*

St. Patrick's Day is celebrated on March 17 in honor of St. Patrick's death on this day in 460. The Irish have observed this holiday for over a thousand years by attending church in the morning and having a festive celebration in the afternoon. St. Patrick's Day was first celebrated in this country in Boston, in 1737. The holiday's first parade in the New World was held in New York City in 1762, and Irish soldiers serving in the English army marched in it.

In the United States, the day and parade were initially motivated by a desire for the Irish to celebrate their heritage. When the Great Potato Famine hit Ireland in 1845, close to a million Irishmen came to America to escape starvation. The St. Patrick's Day parade not only became a time to celebrate their heritage, but also to organize a voting bloc. President Truman attended the New York City St. Patrick's Day parade in 1948.

## EVERYONE'S A LITTLE IRISH ON MARCH 17!

This is now a holiday celebrated by people of all backgrounds in the United States, Canada, and Australia. It has even been celebrated in Japan, Singapore, and Russia. Parades are held not only in New York, but also in Boston, Chicago, Philadelphia, and Savannah. In 1962, the tradition of dying the Chicago River green began as a part of the celebration.

Initially, this was a religious celebration where even the pubs were closed in Ireland on this day until 1970. Now the festivities can easily ignore or put into the distant background the spiritual heritage of this day.

## NOT AN EASY LIFE

St. Patrick brought Christianity to the Irish people in the 400s. His life remains something of a mystery, and some legends that have arisen, like the famous account of his banishing all the snakes from Ireland, are false (Ireland has never had any snakes). He was born in Britain near the end of the fourth century to wealthy parents and died on March 17, 460.

He was taken prisoner at age sixteen by a group of Irish raiders who were seizing his family's estate. They brought him to Ireland where he spent six years in captivity. In his captivity, he worked as a shepherd away from people. In his loneliness and fear he turned to Christ for comfort. It is believed that at this time he began to dream of converting the Irish people to Christ. He escaped from his captivity and walked to the Irish coast and then to Britain where he sensed a call to return to Ireland for missionary work.

## BELOW THE SURFACE

What would be a way to celebrate this holiday and not ignore its spiritual significance? Christ became precious to Patrick when he was lonely and afraid. We can meditate on the testimony of Psalm 34:4: "I sought the Lord, and He answered me, and delivered me from all my fears." At what point of fear do you need to seek God? Also, ask each friend or family member in your celebration how they can be aided in cultivating a closer friendship with Christ next year. Write down their response and read it next St. Patrick's day to see how the year went.

*Celebrating this day is not ultimately about honoring a person, but rather about honoring the person of Christ who gave Patrick a work to do.*

You can also read Ephesians 2:10: "For we are His workmanship, created in Christ Jesus for good works, which God prepared beforehand so that we would walk in them." Pray over each person in your celebration and let each one express their willingness to obey God in regard to His set of good works for them. We are not saved by good works (Ephesians 2:8–9), but we are saved for good works (verse 10). You might even consider beginning to pray for the nations of the world. An excellent resource is *Operation World* by Patrick Johnstone, which gives a way to pray for the nations each day of the year. If you visit operationworld.org, you can be directed to a daily prayer need. This is a key way to celebrate St. Patrick and his legacy.

Celebrating St. Patrick's Day is not ultimately about honoring St. Patrick, but rather about honoring a person of Christ who met him in his fear and gave him a work to do. Why not have a time to worship the Lord and praise Him? Perhaps even use the prayer of St. Patrick and the shorter anthem attributed to him in your worship. Remember, as the early church worshiped the Lord, the first missionary team was called (Acts 13:2–3). Happy St. Patrick's Day!

## PENNY'S Thoughts

As we were growing up, my mother would serve us the traditional Irish dinner of corned beef, cabbage, and potatoes for St. Patrick's Day even though we have no known Irish ancestor. The table was set appropriately with a color theme of green and a shamrock plant as a centerpiece.

Today, in my home, I have kept the green theme but subtracted the menu. Often I have added the reading of *Saint Patrick* by Ann Tompert and illustrated by Michael Garland. It is most enjoyed by those around four through ten years old and is at a third- to fifth-grade reading level. Its themes include missions, persecution, slavery, Ireland, and more. The cover of this book shows St. Patrick holding a shamrock. Tradition says he used the shamrock as an object lesson to illustrate the concept of the Trinity.

You might read it to children with Celtic music playing in the background. If you choose not to serve the corned beef and cabbage, you could make a shamrock shake instead!

I pray God would raise up many in our generation and those to come to love their enemies by sharing the glorious gospel of the Lord Jesus Christ.

# PRACTICAL HELP 17

## An Anthem and Prayer of St. Patrick

Christ be with me, Christ within me, Christ behind me, Christ before me.

Christ beside me, Christ to win me, Christ to comfort me, Christ to restore me.

Christ beneath me, Christ above me, Christ in quiet, Christ in danger,

Christ in hearts of all who love me, Christ in mouth of friend and stranger.

Christ be with me, Christ within me, Christ behind me, and Christ before me.

Christ today and Christ forever, Christ be in my life! Amen!
—Attributed to St. Patrick translated by C. F. Alexander

John Rutter has a wonderful rendition of this anthem on his CD *Gloria*.

## From the Prayer of St. Patrick (St. Patrick's Breastplate)

I arise today
Through a mighty strength, the invocation of the Trinity,
Through belief in the threeness,
Through confession
of the oneness
Of the Creator of Creation.

I arise today
Through the strength of Christ's birth with His baptism,

Through the strength of His crucifixion with His burial,
Through the strength of His resurrection with His ascension,
Through the strength of His descent for the judgment of
Doom. . . .

I arise today
Through God's strength to pilot me:
God's might to uphold me, God's wisdom to guide me,
God's eye to look before me, God's ear to hear me,
God's word to speak for me, God's hand to guard me,
God's way to lie before me, God's shield to protect me,
God's host to save me,
From snares of devils, From temptations and vices,
From everyone who shall wish me ill,
Afar and anear, Alone and in multitude.

I summon today all these powers between me and
those evils,
Against every cruel and merciless power that may oppose my
body and soul,
Against incantations of false prophets, Against black laws of
pagandom,
Against false laws of heretics, Against craft of idolatry,
Against spells of witches and smiths and wizards,
Against every knowledge that corrupts man's body
and soul.

Christ to shield me today
Against poison, against burning, Against drowning, against
wounding,
So that there may come to me abundance of reward.
Christ with me, Christ before me, Christ behind me,
Christ in me, Christ beneath me, Christ above me,
Christ on my right, Christ on my left,
Christ when I lie down, Christ when I sit down, Christ
when I arise,
Christ in the heart of every man who thinks of me,

Christ in the mouth of every person who speaks to me,
Christ in every eye that sees me,
Christ in every ear that hears me.

# PRACTICAL Help 18
## The History of St. Patrick's Day: All Things Irish Quiz

All Things Irish Quiz! Take our quiz below and test your Irish IQ!

I. Some areas in Ireland are known to receive this many inches of rain each year, which accounts for the brilliantly green grass that has earned Ireland the nickname the Emerald Isle:

a) 60   b) 60   c) 80   d) 90

2. "Erin Go Bragh," a phrase heard often on St. Patrick's Day, means:

a) I Love Ireland          b) Ireland Forever
c) Brave and Free          d) Ireland, My Home

3. Irish tradition says that anyone who kisses the Blarney Stone, which is located near this town, will be blessed with the Irish gift of gab:

a) Dublin   b) Wexford   c) Cork   d) Waterford

4. This Nobel Prize–winning Irish poet and playwright was also a senator of the Irish Free State from 1922 to 1928:

a) George Bernard Shaw   b) James Joyce
c) Jonathan Swift          d) William Butler Yeats

5. This film, shot in Ireland in 1952, was directed by John Ford:

a) *Ryan's Daughter*       b) *The Quiet Man*
c) *The Dead*              d) *The Informer*

6. Traditional Irish music has found an international audience with the popularity of such Celtic bands as:

a) The Chieftains          b) The Lads
c) Shannon Rovers          d) Sweet Honey in the Rock

7. In November 1995, the people of Ireland narrowly passed a referendum legalizing:

   a) same-sex marriages      b) abortion
   c) divorce                 d) marijuana

8. With 27,136 square miles of land, the Republic of Ireland is approximately half the size of this U.S. state:

   a) Montana                 b) California
   c) Louisiana               d) Arkansas

9. Today, this number of Americans trace their ancestry back to Ireland:

   a) 10 million              b) 25 million
   c) 40 million              d) 65 million

## Answers

I. d; 2. b; 3. c; 4. d; 5. b; 6. a; 7. c; 8. d; 9. c

Source: history.com

Chapter
Twenty-Three

Arbor Day:
*Caring for
God's Creation*

## "And all the trees of
the field will clap their hands!"

This picturesque verse (Isaiah 55:12) is just one of the many verses in the Bible that use the image of trees, either literally or figuratively. Psalm 1 tells us that the righteous "are like trees planted along the riverbank, bearing fruit each season. Their leaves never wither, and they prosper in all they do" (verse 3 NLT).

### OUR CREATIVE MAKER

Genesis 1 tells us seven times as God created the heavens and the earth that "it was good." Although you're probably familiar with the biblical account of creation, take some time to reread this chapter. Try reading it in a couple of translations and enjoy the various cadences different versions employ. This activity will freshen your appreciation for what our Creator has done, and is especially effective with school-age children.

We learn in Genesis 2:9 (NLT) that the "Lord God made all sorts of trees grow up from the ground—trees that were beautiful and that produced delicious fruit." This is typical of God's ability and His provision: making trees that are both beautiful to look at and that grow fruit to nourish us.

### "HOW DOES YOUR GARDEN GROW?"

In the nursery rhyme, Mary Contrary's garden grows with silver bells and cockleshells, but in real life, a garden needs tending—planting at the right time and in the right way, fertilizing and weeding, and so on. How does God expect His beautiful creation to be cared for? The answer is found in the first chapter of Genesis.

God blessed them; and God said to them, "Be fruitful and multiply, and fill the earth, and subdue it and rule over the fish of the sea and over the birds of the sky and over every living thing that moves on the earth." (1:28)

It is to human beings—God's highest creation, the only aspect of creation that has been made in the image of God—that He gives charge over His world. Psalm 8:6–8 tells us that everything has been put under the feet of mankind; therefore we have a God-given responsibility to care for the earth He has given to us.

## THE ROOTS OF ARBOR DAY

As Christians, we of course do not worship trees or shrubs or flowers or anything else in creation—we reserve praise for their Creator. But being mindful of our charge to oversee the natural world, a day such as Arbor Day is a welcome time to celebrate what our Creator has done and to take tangible steps to tend His earth.

Perhaps you've heard of Julius Sterling Morton (his son Joy founded the Morton Salt Company). In 1854, he and his wife, Caroline Joy, moved from Michigan to what was then the Nebraska Territory. When they first came west where he would take a position with the Nebraska City News, they found grassy prairies and very few trees. The Mortons were nature lovers who planted flowers and shrubs around their home, but they and other pioneers missed the beauty of the landscape filled with trees they had known back east. Not only were trees beautiful, but they offered benefits to the land—with gusts of wind sweeping across the plains and blowing about the fertile topsoil, the land was not naturally conducive to farming. Trees would act as windbreaks to hold down and thus conserve soil, and also would be useful as building material, fuel, shade, and fruit.

*Not only are trees beautiful, but they offer benefits to the land.*

The Mortons began with three hundred apple trees and soon followed with more than a thousand additional trees planted on their land.

Morton also used his position at the newspaper to promote the planting of trees. He learned and reported what trees were well suited to Nebraska's climate and encouraged other settlers to plant. J. Sterling Morton's overall influence in Nebraska rose. He was elected to the territory's legislative assembly and appointed secretary; he also served as acting governor. On January 4, 1872, Morton, as a member of the Nebraska Board of Agriculture, spoke to the group about the importance of tree planting. He proposed naming April 10, 1872 as the first Arbor Day—and more than a million trees were planted across Nebraska on that day!

Today Arbor Day is officially observed in all fifty states on the last Friday in April, though its actual date may vary by state depending on the best time to plant trees in any particular region's climate.

## TREES IN THE BIBLE

How can we commemorate Arbor Day? One way is to examine trees that are mentioned in the Bible.

**Cedar:** Do you have a cedar chest or anything else made of cedar? If you do, you know how distinctively fragrant this wood is. Cedars from Israel's neighbor Lebanon were used by Solomon in the construction of the temple. You can read about this in 1 Kings 6 and 7.

Cedar is also used figuratively in Scripture. In Hosea 14, the Lord speaks of healing Israel and then she will have deep roots like the cedars of Lebanon (verse 5) and "its branches will spread out like beautiful olive trees, as fragrant as the cedars of Lebanon" (verse 6 NLT). Psalm 92:12 NLT says, "The godly will flourish like palm trees and grow strong like the cedars of Lebanon."

**Fig:** We're all familiar with Adam and Eve's use of fig leaves (see Genesis 3:7 for a refresher), but the fig is referenced many other times in the Bible. One story that generates some good discussion is Jesus' cursing of the fig tree in Matthew 21:18–20.

Jesus uses the fig as an example of watching for signs of the times (Mark 13:28), and James uses the fig (3:12) to make a point about the source of disparate things. The fig symbolizes a time of prosperity in 1 Kings 4:25 and helps exemplify faithfulness in difficulties in the great passage beginning with Habakkuk 3:17.

*The olive tree in Scripture reminds us of faithfulness, steadfastness, continuity, peace, and anointing.*

**Almond:** When Jacob directed his sons to pack a bag of presents to take to Egypt, he chose to send gifts that were not produced in that country—almonds were in the package (Genesis 43:11). Almonds also appeared on Aaron's rod (Numbers 17:8) and are referenced in other passages such as Ecclesiastes 12:5 and Jeremiah 1:11.

**Olive:** Jesus' custom was to spend time on the Mount of Olives (Luke 22:39). David speaks of himself as an "olive tree in the house of God" (Psalm 52:8), and Noah's dove returned to him with an olive leaf (Genesis 8:11), which let him know that floodwaters were receding. The olive tree in Scripture reminds us of faithfulness, steadfastness, continuity, peace, and anointing. Several ancient olive trees, some over two thousand years old, still flourish in Galilee.[1]

Other trees mentioned in the Bible include the acacia, cypress, mulberry, myrtle, pal, pomegranate, poplar, sycamore, terebinth, and willow. You might enjoy looking up passages that refer to these and other trees and determining where they are referred to literally, figuratively, or both.

## MEANINGFUL ARBOR DAY ACTIVITIES

Obviously, planting trees is at the crux of Arbor Day. You might work with your church, a civic organization, or other neighborhood group to decide what kinds of trees you can help plant and where. Visit www.arborday.org for information on ordering trees that would grow well in your area. Some families have planted a tree as a memorial to a loved one.

Walk through a park or a forest with a tree identification book. The variety of trees you discover might surprise you!

Take a guided hike at a nature center or at a state park. Many state parks have activities especially for children.

Extend caring for God's creation beyond Arbor Day. Ask your local government if your church can organize a pick-up-trash-in-the-park day. Encourage members of your church to recycle. Some churches have recycling bins in their parking lots where they collect newspapers and other materials, but if this is not feasible for your situation, you might set up a receptacle for pop cans and offer to redeem them, and use the money for a church project.

Offer to help plant annuals around your church grounds. Are there people in your church family or among your neighbors who would enjoy flowers and greenery, but who cannot physically dig holes and plant? They would appreciate your help.

Read President Theodore Roosevelt's proclamation about Arbor Day on page 212. Are his words from 1907 relevant today? In what way? How might his message be different if it were delivered today?

Enjoy the tree trivia and quiz on page 213. What facts could you add? Make up your own quiz and see how well family members or classmates do on it.

Read some of the many passages in Scripture about God's creation, e.g., Psalms 24:1–2; 33:5–6; 89:11; 104:10–14. What other verses can you find? Talk with your family and friends about the relationship between the Creator and His creation.

Read Psalm 148:9 and discuss: How can "fruit trees and all cedars" praise the Lord?

How is wisdom a tree of life? See Proverbs 3:18.

NOTE
1. http://www.sooperarticles.com/art-entertainment-articles/movies-tv-articles/amazing-olive-tree-its-biblical-history-35482.html

## PRACTICAL Help 19

### A Proclamation
by President Theodore Roosevelt, 1907

To the School Children of the United States: Arbor Day (which means simply "Tree Day") is now observed in every State in our Union and mainly in the schools. At various times from January to December, but chiefly in this month of April, you give a day or part of a day to special exercises and perhaps to actual tree planting, in recognition of the importance of trees to us as a Nation, and of what they yield in adornment, comfort, and useful products to the communities in which you live.

It is well that you should celebrate your Arbor Day thoughtfully, for within your lifetime the Nation's need of trees will become serious. We of an older generation can get along without what we have, though with growing hardship; but in your full manhood and womanhood you will want what nature once so bountifully supplied, and man so thoughtlessly destroyed; and because of that want you will reproach us, not for what we have used, but for what we have wasted.

For the nation as for the man or woman, and the boy or girl, the road to success is the right use of what we have and the improvement of present opportunity. If you neglect to prepare yourselves not for the duties and responsibilities which will fall upon you later, if you do not learn the things which you will need to know when your school days are over, you will, suffer the consequences. So any nation that in its youth lives only for the day, reaps without sowing, and consumes without husbanding, must expect the penalty of the prodigal, whose labor could with difficulty find him the bare means of life. A people without children would face a hopeless future; a country without trees is almost as hopeless; forests which are so used that they can not renew themselves will soon vanish, and with them all their benefits. A true forest is not merely a storehouse full of wood, but, as it were, a factory of wood, and at the same time a reservoir of water. When you help to preserve our forests or, to plant new ones you are acting the part of good citizens. The value of forestry deserves, therefore, to be taught in the schools, which aim to make good citizens of you. If your Arbor Day exercises help you to realize what benefits each one of you receives from the forests, and how by your assistance these benefits may continue, they will serve a good end.

# PRACTICAL Help 20
## Did You Know?

- The most popular state tree is the sugar maple—New York, West Virginia, Wisconsin, and Vermont.
- The oak is the official national tree for the United States.
- One tree produces about 260 pounds of oxygen per year.
- Over the course of its life, a single tree can absorb one ton of carbon dioxide.
- Native Americans used the red cedar tree to make canoes, and also wove its bark into baskets, fishing nets, and fabric.
- Parts of trees are found in tires, chewing gum, hair spray, shampoo, paint, toothpaste, and more.

## Tree Quiz

1. What is the most common tree in the United States?
2. What is the largest tree by volume?

3. What is the tallest species of tree in the world?

4. What tree was nearly wiped out by a Dutch disease?

5. What kind of tree did Isaac Newton sit under when he discovered gravity?

6. In what kind of tree was the partridge found in "The Twelve Days of Christmas"?

7. What kind of tree is most likely to be struck by lightning?

   a. redwood        b. oak            c. silver maple
   d. elm            e. sequoia        f. apple
   g. pear

## Answers

I. c; 2. e; 3. a; 4. d; 5. f; 6. g; 7. b

Sources:
arborday.org/kids/treetrivia
idahoforests.org
usna.usda.gov/Gardens/collections/statetreetrivia.html
savatree.com/tree-facts.html

**Chapter Twenty-Four**

# Mother's Day and Father's Day (and Grandparent's Day!)

*Honoring Your Lord as You Honor Your Heritage*

Anna Jarvis in Philadelphia led a campaign to celebrate a national Mother's Day. She first persuaded her church in West Virginia to celebrate it on the second anniversary of her mother's death. The first official Mother's Day was on May 10, 1908, in Philadelphia. Later, President Woodrow Wilson proclaimed the second Sunday of May as Mother's Day. Today it has become a celebration in countries all over the world.

Sonora Dodd came up with the idea of Father's Day as she was listening to a Mother's Day sermon. She desired to honor her father who had raised her after her mother's death. The first Father's Day was celebrated on June 19, 1910. Later President Calvin Coolidge proclaimed the third Sunday in June as the official Father's Day holiday.

## PONDERING GOD'S
## PROVIDENCE IN YOUR HERITAGE

As a believer celebrates and seeks to honor the Lord on these special days—Mother's Day, Father's Day, and even Grandparent's Day, which is the first Sunday after Labor Day—he can take time to ponder God's sovereign hand in his life.

Mark Ashton-Smith, a thirty-three-year-old lecturer at Cambridge University, capsized in treacherous waters while he was kayaking off the Isle of Wright in England. Clinging to his craft, he reached for his cell phone to call his father who was four thousand miles away training British troops in Dubai. At once his father relayed his son's call for help to the Coast Guard who had an installation less than a mile from his son's accident. In less than twelve minutes he was rescued. Mark quickly thought to call his dad.

Whether or not your first instinct is to call your father or mother will depend on your relationship to them. George Washington spoke of his mother as the most beautiful woman he had ever seen. Abraham Lincoln attributed all that he was to his "angel mother" whose prayers clung to him all his life.

*Seeing life from God's point of view is a mark of wisdom.*

But what if you cannot identify with their glowing compliments of a mother or father? I remember reading the testimony of a woman who was raised by an alcoholic father and a mother who would inexplicably erupt in anger like a dormant volcano. She found it ever difficult to sit through a sermon about godly parents or God as a heavenly Father because of her feelings of condemnation and guilt. In her mind God was not righteous, faithful, and true but unreliable, irrational, and unpredictable. She never knew when she would get hugged or slapped and could not figure out the reason for either one.

Seeing life from God's point of view is a mark of wisdom. Our perspective can lie in faith in a sovereign and good God or it can be rooted in unbelief. Dr. Paul Vitz, a professor of psychology at New York University, has written a book entitled *Faith of the Fatherless*. His thesis is that atheists have a deep psychological need to reject God because of their bad relationship with their earthly father. The disappointment and feeling of rejection by their own father unconsciously justifies their rejection of God. He cites numerous examples such as Madalyn Murray O'Hair, the woman responsible for getting the Supreme Court to ban prayer in the public schools. She hated her father so much that she once tried to kill him with a butcher knife. The French philosopher Voltaire, a powerful critic of Christianity, hated his abusive father so much that he changed his family name. Joseph Stalin was repeatedly beaten by his father, and Adolph Hitler's father has been described as authoritative, selfish, and hard. If any of us project the imperfection of our earthly father onto God, we are lacking God's wisdom and will reach some very wrong conclusions.

You can get further insight into this in *The Making of an Atheist* by James S. Spiegel.

## HONORING THE ONE PERFECT FATHER

I received an assignment to write an article for a publication pertaining to some aspect of fathering. After running a complete printout of every reference to the word "father" in the Bible, I looked up each reference and attempted to collate my findings. This study led me to write an article on "The One Perfect Father— God." That seemed to be the message of the Bible.

George MacDonald had a wonderful childhood and found great refuge in his loving father. However, he gave some profound advice for those who find no pleasure, warmth, or love in the name "father." He states, "You must interpret the word by all that you missed in life. All that human tenderness can give or devise in the nearness and readiness of love, all and infinitely more must be true of the perfect Father of the maker and fatherhood."

All of us need to take seriously MacDonald's advice as we celebrate these special holidays of honoring our parents. No one has ever had a sinless heritage since Adam, the first father, fell into sin. However, while our heritage is not perfect in being sinless, it is perfect in God's design to lead us to a revelation of the one perfect Father. Go to Him and let Him heal you from the hurts of your past. Let His truth uproot any lies so that you can begin to view yourself as one for whom He gave His greatest sacrifice—His Son—in order to have an intimate relationship with you. When we begin to see Him for who He really is, our relationship with Him is what will give meaning to every aspect of our lives.

On every holiday that causes you to honor your heritage, remember to ponder His providential provision with the wisdom of both a sovereign and good God. May His wisdom lead you to thank Him that this is the means to ultimately reveal to you Himself—the one Perfect Father. There may be intense joy in your heritage, or pain—or both—but the goal is to see His love, which is superior to the best of any person.

For my father and my mother have forsaken me,
But the Lord will take me up. (Psalm 27:10)

But Zion said, "The Lord has forsaken me,
And the Lord has forgotten me."
"Can a woman forget her nursing child
And have no compassion on the son of her womb?
Even these may forget, but I will not forget you.
"Behold, I have inscribed you on the palms *of My hands;*
Your walls are continually before Me." (Isaiah 49:14–16)

Be open to including others in your celebration, such as singles or couples who have no children. On one Mother's Day, I passed out 3 x 5 cards to every guest and asked them to write down two valuable lessons they had learned from their mother. Each guest was allowed to talk about his or her mother, so each person participated in the celebration. All may not be a mother, but nearly all of us have or have had a mother. After reading each card, I let people guess who was being honored by the compliment I read. I then gave the cards to each mother who was present and the other cards were sent to every living mother who had been honored that day.

> *There is no greater way to honor a father or mother than to pray over them and to also pray for their children.*

There is no greater way to honor a father or mother than to pray over them and to also pray for their children. The father or mother will feel their arms being lifted up and their burdens being lightened. Once again, this is a way that one who does not have children can vitally enter into the celebration. At times, I have passed out key Scriptures to guide the prayers.

On one Father's Day, we let each father who was present share his vision for each of his children. It gave him a time to affirm them and gave them hope in regard to their future. A Mother's or Father's Day can be much more than simply receiving flowers or a new tie. They can be life-changing events.

## PENNY'S Thoughts

The celebrations Bill just described are precious jeweled memories to me, especially now that my father has gone to be with the Lord. May God grant you wonderful celebrations that honor your parents or those who have played that role in your life. Ask God for wisdom in how they would feel most honored. Here are a few ideas:

- Have the children and/or grandchildren put on "This is Your Life." Have individuals act out or describe different scenes from the father's or mother's, grandfather's or grandmother's life. End with each individual sharing one or two things she appreciates in them. Close in prayer, thanking God for their lives and asking God to continue to bless them.

- Write a letter to your parents, highlighting special memories and investments they have made in your life. End with a Bible verse you are praying for them at this time in their lives.

- Any praise you might receive throughout the year, deflect it by giving God and your parents the credit for the investments they have made in your lives. Afterwards, jot them a quick note or e-mail telling them how their influence has made you successful.

- Practically speaking, for older parents and aging grandparents, you might plan a work day at their house. Ask for a list of projects ahead of time so the day can be well planned. Consider people in your church who might not have family in the area.

- Make a big, double-sided banner for their yard; string it from tree to tree—"Thanks for being such a loving grandmother!"

Chapter
Twenty-Five

Memorial Day,
Veterans Day,
and the
Fourth of July:

*"Protect Us by Thy Might,
Great God, Our King!"*

There are several days on the calendar year that celebrate the freedom of the United States and the debt that many have paid to secure that freedom. The most notable is the Fourth of July. This holiday celebrates the signing of the Declaration of Independence on July 4, 1776, when we mark the birth of our country.

Memorial Day is a time to commemorate those who have served in the armed forces and to honor those who have died to keep our nation free. It was originally called Decoration Day and first observed on May 30, 1868, to honor those who had died in the Civil War. The name was changed to Memorial Day in 1882 and expanded to honor soldiers who had died in other wars as well. Memorial Day was declared an official federal holiday in 1971 and is celebrated on the first Monday in May.

Veterans Day is yet another national holiday that is a tribute to all the men and women who have defended our nation's cause of freedom in the world and celebrated on November 11. Armed Forces Day salutes those serving in the various branches of the military. It was declared a holiday by President Truman in 1950 and is celebrated on the third Saturday in May.

## A GREAT HERITAGE

Though the United States has never had an official religion, it is undeniable that the roots of our nation are of the Judeo-Christian tradition. One of our strengths as a country is that we do not rely on the government to declare what our religious beliefs should be, but instead hold on to the right to practice religion freely. Our founders, while rightly refraining from establishing a religion, correctly understood that a nation that ignored God's principles would not flourish. "It is impossible to rightly govern the world without God and the Bible," George Washington declared.

The great revolutionary statesman Patrick Henry believed "There is a just God that presides over the destinies of nations."

Calvin Coolidge, president from 1923–1929, wrote, "The foundations of our society and our government rest so much on the

teachings of the Bible that it would be difficult to support them if
faith in these teachings would cease to
be practically universal in our
country."

*"It is impossible to rightly govern the world without God and the Bible,"* George Washington declared.

Many of our traditional
patriotic songs acknowledge
God and ask for His favor.
Do you recognize which
songs contain these lines?

"Long may our land be
bright with freedom's holy
light; Protect us by Thy might,
Great God, our King!"[1]

"Stand beside her and guide her,
through the night with a light from above."[2]

"America! America! God shed His grace on thee."[3]

"And this be our motto: 'In God is our trust.'"[4]

## THANKING GOD FOR OUR FREEDOM

One way to more fully appreciate our heritage as a free people
is to learn about societies that do not enjoy the freedoms we take
for granted. Not all nations grant their citizens the right to peace-
fully protest, and in some countries, in which the press is controlled
by the government, a person would not be able to write a letter to
the editor of the newspaper and present a viewpoint on a current
issue. Some countries block use of the Internet in an attempt to
control information that its citizens are exposed to.

As Christians, we need to be aware of and thankful for our
freedom to worship as we choose. Not all believers around the
world enjoy this right. You can learn more about Christians in
difficult circumstances worldwide through Voice of the Martyrs
(www.persecution.com).

Another way to embrace our heritage as a free people is to
examine our freedom in Christ. Whatever political or national

climate in which we find ourselves, our true freedom comes from the source—Jesus Christ. Every gift, including political freedom, is a gift from God (James 1:17). A believer's acknowledgment of Christ is also recognition of His provision of spiritual freedom. One can live in a country that guarantees certain freedoms and yet live in spiritual bondage. On the other hand, one can live under political oppression and experience true freedom. Only when Jesus makes us free will we be "free indeed" (John 8:36).

## A STIRRING MOMENT

One of my former students shared this story:

On the first really hot day of the year I visited a small town church of no more than a hundred people. As the county sheriff gave the weekly announcements, he welcomed a recently returned veteran home from the front lines. The congregation stood and applauded, turning in the direction of the young father. He sat upright and reserved—a real, live hero.

When asked to share some stories from "over there," the corporal told of his birthday a few months prior, his tour as a Humvee gunner, and the rocket that struck his convoy. And then in the same breath he thanked the congregation, the family of God, for watching over and taking care of his family while he was away. He proceeded to tell several stories of everyday heroism there, in that small town, which freed him to be their hero on the other side of the world.

A scene like this could be repeated throughout our country as our men and women return from service or come home on leave. This particular soldier served in Iraq. Today we have troops in many locations around the world, some on active duty, and many available to be deployed when needed. In addition to protecting our country in times of war and aiding in peacekeeping missions, our military often joins in disaster relief efforts both at home and abroad.

*A nation needs principled leaders, and it needs people of faith to be in prayer.*

A nation needs principled leaders, and it needs people of faith to be in prayer. However, it is the ordinary men and women whose daily lives have been given to service that make our country the beacon of hope it is.

You'll see some practical, hands-on ideas below for commemorating our nation, especially on patriotic holidays. Take time to thank God for the great opportunity He has given us. Make it your purpose to pray regularly for our country throughout the year, and ask the Lord to lead you into a greater experience into the freedom you have in Christ.

NOTES
1. "My Country, 'Tis of Thee"
2. "God Bless America"
3. "O Beautiful for Spacious Skies"
4. "The Star Spangled Banner"

## PENNY'S Thoughts

I remember one special evening a veteran came to our home to share his testimony with our father/son club. He had been a chaplain during the Vietnam War. God miraculously spared his life in the heat of an incredibly intense battle. Every detail was spellbinding. The boys came away with another treasured, real-life story of the providence of God in one of His children's lives. His wife commemorates the anniversary of the day his life was spared with a huge bouquet of yellow roses—his favorite.

In our town, the Memorial Day Parade is my favorite. I enjoy the patriotic music and the chance to honor our veterans. It is also a wonderful way to build patriotism in our children and to model gratefulness for those who have served in the armed forces. We always stand when the American flag passes by and stand and applaud our veterans in the parade.

Go to YouTube and search for "Memorial Day Tribute"—many wonderful and moving tributes will come up. On some of them, the Armed Forces medley is played and sung. This is a fine way for children to learn the lyrics and melodies of these great songs.

If you have a veteran in your life or someone currently serving in the armed forces, take time to pray for them and thank them for their sacrifice for our freedom. Inviting veterans to dinner and having them share their experience is memorable. I prize the DVD of my father recalling his historic flight over Germany in WWII. This is a treasured gift to pass down from generation to generation.

## PRACTICAL Help 21

### Patriotism: Here are some ways to honor active servicemen and women and veterans:

- Search the Internet or contact a local military base to find an organization that helps returning veterans with practical needs. Doing so is giving "a cup of cold water" in Jesus' name (Matthew 10:42). Even if your gift is anonymous, He will see it.

- Have you ever come upon a group of active servicemen or women in a museum or other public place? Go up to them and thank them for their service. They will appreciate it!

- Find out who from your church is active. Get your youth group or Bible study to write letters of encouragement, or send care packages: toiletries, word search books, snacks such as trail mix, and so on. NOTE: In most cases, you cannot send these items to a recruit who is in basic training or boot camp. Check with the person's family or a recruiting office first.

- If you live nearby, contact a military base and let them know how many guys or gals you can host for a holiday or Sunday afternoon dinner. They would enjoy a home-cooked meal and company with their buddies away from base.
- Ask your children's teacher to invite a veteran to their classroom.
- Invite the family of a deployed serviceman/woman for supper.
- Buy paper poppies from veterans around Memorial Day.

## Other ideas for patriotic celebrations:

- Discover the history and meaning of our nation's symbols: the flag, eagle, Liberty Bell, the Great Seal, Uncle Sam.
- Visit or learn about Mount Rushmore, and war memorials (World War II, Korean, Vietnam). The moving Vietnam wall is a replica of the memorial in Washington, D.C., and travels around the country. Check the schedule at www.themovingwall.org.
- Find out about tributes to great Americans: the Lincoln Memorial, the Jefferson Memorial, the Washington Monument.
- Depending on your children's ages, read and review all or portions of great American documents: The Declaration of Independence, the preamble to the Constitution, the Gettysburg Address.

## To discuss:

- How did the Christian faith of leaders such as Abraham Lincoln and John Witherspoon influence their choices and the lives of others? (John Witherspoon was a Christian minister who became president of the College of New Jersey in 1768.)
- In what ways can we as Christians be good citizens? (possible answers depending on age and maturity: keep parks and sidewalks clean, be a good neighbor, obey the law, respect police officers, display the flag, vote, keep informed about current

events, pray for our leaders, encourage our elected officials when they make principled decisions, stand against evil, be involved in a civic organization)

- Let your celebration of this "freedom" holiday include a time of prayer to God that He would lead you and your loved ones into a greater freedom to worship and serve God as they live out His unique plan for them. See pages 31–34 in my book *Living the Life God Has Planned*, which explain the idea of being "free from man" and overcoming peer dependence.

- For teens and adults: Talk about the book *When a Nation Forgets God* by Erwin Lutzer.

Chapter
Twenty-Six

Labor Day:
*Honoring the
Lord in
Your Work*

L abor Day is a holiday that is celebrated in many industrialized nations to honor working men and women of their country. In the United States—as well as in Canada—it is celebrated on the first Monday in September. Congress declared it a national holiday in 1894, and presently it is a legal holiday in every state in the Union including the District of Columbia. There is a special significance that this day should have in the heart of a Christian and understanding this will aid his or her celebration.

## DELIGHT IN GOD AND HIS WORK

The Bible is the written record of God's revelation to man. It begins with God's work of creation. While God rested from His work of creation on the seventh day, He continues to work all things after the counsel of His will by ruling and overruling every circumstance of life for His glory and the ultimate good of His people.

> Having been predestined according to His purpose who works all things after the counsel of His will. (Ephesians 1:11b)

> And we know that God causes all things to work together for good to those who love God, to those who are called according to His purpose. (Romans 8:28)

God is actively at work in His people (Philippians 2:13), and believers in Christ are called His workmanship (Ephesians 2:10). Take time to adore God for His work of creation, salvation, and His daily providential work in your life.

> Great are the works of the Lord;
> They are studied by all who delight in them. (Psalm 111:2)

## SEE WORK AS A BLESSING

Work is not to be viewed as a chore but as a blessing and gift of God. In fact work was a part of God's creation before the fall of man. It is part of the original paradise in the garden of Eden.

Then the Lord God took the man and put him into the Garden of Eden to cultivate it and keep it. (Genesis 2:15)

The Hebrew word for "put" comes from a root word meaning "to rest." When you are doing God's work in the place of His assignment, one can know a rest in the soul. All of Adam's life in the garden was viewed as a holy service to God.

One's workplace is a place not only to do a job, but to do one's job "with God." When one becomes a Christian, the general advice is to remain in one's present state and job unless God clearly calls one out of it.

Each one is to remain with God in that condition in which he was called. (1 Corinthians 7:24)

The key phrase that sticks out to me is "with God." This advice was originally given to a slave. Since sin has entered the world, work is now called "toil" (Genesis 3:17). Likewise, the "thorns and thistles" from the entrance of sin into the world make work more challenging. God can still glorify His name and enable you to experience His promises as you work. Take time to ask God for His viewpoint of your job.

## PRESENT THE DAYS OF YOUR LIFE TO GOD

Every individual in life is a servant. Whether or not it is a good thing to be a servant depends on who you have as a master. The one who declares "I am not a servant to anyone; I do whatever I please," is professing their slavery to sin, their own self will

(Romans 6:17), and ultimately to Satan (John 8:34, 44).

It is a great privilege to live as a servant of Jesus Christ, because HE is a Master that loves us and died for us to know true freedom (Galatians 2:20). He has set us free from sin so that we can now present our lives and all the capacities of our life to Him to use for His righteous purposes (Romans 6:11–13).

There is great freedom in taking time to renew your presentation of the days of your life to God for Him to fill them with that which brings the greatest glory to Him, benefit to others, and satisfaction to you. God takes care of what is committed to Him (2 Timothy 1:12). Service is simply doing the work that He has given us to do.

I glorified You on the earth, having accomplished the work which You have given Me to do. (John 17:4)

## REALIZING THE RESPONSIBILITY AND PURPOSES OF WORK

The refusal of an able-bodied man to work and provide for his family is cited as disorderly conduct (2 Thessalonians 3:6, 11). It is even given as a ground for church discipline (see verses 6, 14). Such irresponsible behavior is clearly against the practice and precepts of the apostles.

The practice of the apostle Paul was one of diligent labor and willing service. While it is not wrong for a minister to get paid for his labor (1 Timothy 5:18), Paul gave up this right in order not to be a burden to anyone, to show that his motivation for service was not money, and to provide an example for hard work (1 Corinthians 9:3–14; 2 Thessalonians 3:8–9). However, it is perfectly clear that the one who refuses to work should not be supported if their need is due to their own slothfulness (2 Thessalonians 3:10).

*An honest worker is a testimony to the unbelieving world.*

The refusal to work tends to make one a "busy body." This term describes an individual who pursues useless, superfluous, and meddlesome activities (2 Thessalonians 3:11; cf. 1 Timothy 5:13). For this reason, Paul exhorted the Thessalonian church with the words, "to make it your ambition to lead a quiet life and attend to your own business and work with your hands" (1 Thessalonians 4:11). The Greek word translated "to make it your ambition" means to "aspire to something and to eagerly strive for it." A "quiet life" refers to a calm, restful spirit and peace of mind. This kind of life is coupled with being faithful to God in the performance of one's own tasks. Diligent labor is a way in which every person can serve God. A "pious" idle person can do great damage to the Lord's cause. On the other hand an honest worker is a testimony to the unbelieving world (verse 12).

One legitimate purpose for work is to provide for one's own needs and that of one's family (verse 12). To fail to provide for one's own family is a denial of the faith and a great hindrance to one's testimony (1 Timothy 5:8). This purpose to provide for oneself and family in an honest manner also overflows into the purpose of being able to give to others in need (Ephesians 4:28). Take time on Labor Day to praise God for His grace that provides the motivation and enablement for your work. Also thank Him for His provisions and ask Him for His wisdom in being a steward of these provisions.

## MOTIVATION FOR WORK

James Winship tells of a traffic flagman exhibiting great joy as he endured the hot July sun as well as angry gestures from the frustrated and impatient commuters. He enthusiastically extended friendly greetings to the passing motorists. James, astonished by this workman's attitude, rolled down his window and asked him for his secret. "I'm happy because I'm not working for the man," he shouted, but "I'm a flagman for Jesus!"[1] The highest motivation for one's work is to bring pleasure to Christ. Even a first-century slave is commanded to do his service for Christ and not ultimately for men (Ephesians 6:5–7; Colossians 3:22–23).

The secret of good workmanship is not only better pay and more benefits. The secret of good workmanship is when it is done for the Lord from the heart. This is the primary way that believers can accomplish God's will for their lives (Ephesians 6:6). It has been said that we do not need people who do extraordinary things as much as we need people who do ordinary things extraordinarily well for the glory of God. Providing meals for the family can be done for Christ, as is diligent and skillful office work. A mail carrier can deliver his mail for Christ, and a teacher can teach her students for Christ. All that a believer does is to be done for the glory of God (1 Corinthians 10:31). This simply means that our work is to draw attention to the revealed attributes of God. This is the secret of good workmanship.

A believer is to do his or her work "in the name of the Lord Jesus" (Colossians 3:17). The "name of Jesus" refers to His character, His reputation, and His authority. Our work is to be done in such a way that it displays Jesus' character and enhances His reputation as we depend upon His authority and enablement to do it. James Winship began sharing his faith with his fellow worker after securing his dream job of being a big city police officer. As he began to share Christ with his sergeant, he was interrupted with the question, "What kind of police officer are you going to be?" After James replied, "I don't know yet," the sergeant exclaimed, "When and if you prove yourself to be a good cop, then you can come and talk to me about God." When James was named officer of the year after his second year of work, the sergeant congratulated him and told him he was ready to talk about

*Jesus spent most of His brief life on earth in a carpenter shop.*

God. James did his work "in the name of the Lord Jesus."

## ACCEPT GOD'S PLAN FOR WORK

Work is not something that is evil or something to be avoided. View your daily occupation as what you do for the Lord each day, no matter how menial or routine it may be. No work should be considered menial, but rather as an essential part of making the world run smoothly. Remember that Jesus spent most of His brief life on earth in a carpenter shop (Mark 6:3).

In God's infinite wisdom He has provided work as a part of mankind's role in this world (Psalm 104:14–24). It was a part of His plan before and after the entrance of sin into the world. The presence of sin not only makes a person's work more difficult but also resulted in the temptation to make work an idol. When this is the case, one lives for their work—for the money made, for esteem—rather than for the Lord. One gracious provision of God is the Sabbath principle that God gave to regulate our work. It is an opportunity to rest and worship and an aid to remember that work is a gift of God and to be done for Christ.

## ANTICIPATE REWARD FOR YOUR WORK

In order to get a proper understanding of your work, one must view it from the perspective of eternity. From a worldly viewpoint one may look at their work as frustrating and meaningless. It's not only that we should be reliable to work diligently and honestly at a job, but that the job itself matters. The believer in Christ is assured, however, that any work done for Him will be rewarded (Ephesians 6:8; Colossians 3:24–25). "God is not unjust so as to forget your work" (Hebrews 6:10). Any work done for Christ will never be forgotten (Mark 9:41).

Everyone will give an account to the Lord for their work. As God assured first-century slaves that He would remember their work, he also reminded their masters that they too have a Master in heaven to whom they will give account (Colossians 4:1). An

employer will be held accountable for not paying a fair wage to his employee (cf. Malachi 3:5). A believer's work will be evaluated by a gracious, good, and omniscient God. All that is done in faith and motivated by love will be remembered for all eternity (1 Corinthians 3:11–15; 13:1–3).
One's work must be done in dependence on the Lord.

I am the vine, you are the branches; he who abides in Me and I in him, he bears much fruit, for apart from Me you can do nothing. (John 15:5)

Unless the Lord builds the house,
They labor in vain who build it;
Unless the Lord guards the city,
The watchman keeps awake in vain. (Psalm 127:1)

We are to labor in His strength with our anxieties cast upon Him (Philippians 4:6–7; Colossians 1:29). Such is the work of faith and labor of love (1 Thessalonians 1:3).

## ANTICIPATE JOYFUL WORK FOR ALL ETERNITY

"Secular" work can be holy service to the Lord. In this present age God's will is to scatter His people to be salt and light in a variety of legitimate vocations. The work itself is holy service to the Lord, as well as an opportunity to be salt and light. People who believe their work is important have the most job satisfaction. See Ecclesiastes 5:18–20 where we learn that enjoyment of our work is a gift from God. If we are not doing everything as though to the Lord (see Colossians 3:17), our work will be an eternal waste, no matter how rich or famous we may become. However, if we seek to work for Jesus, we can know joy and satisfaction in our labor.

Our work is also to prepare us to serve Christ for all eternity (Revelation 22:3). We will then be able to serve Him day and night

(7:15). Heaven is not described as a place when work will be absent. It is described as a place of joy (Psalm 16:11), and part of this joy will be the joy of work.

Happy Labor Day!

## PENNY'S Thoughts

What a great holiday to remind us to thank those who have provided for us by their labor. Children can write notes of gratefulness to their parents and/or their teachers. Children might need help in visualizing how their parents' work benefits them.

You might have a conversation with younger children asking them how they picture their mom's and/or dad's work. Explain when the parent must wake up, how they get to work, where they go when they get there—do they sit, stand? Do they wear special clothing?

For an older child, you can elaborate on what preparation was needed to obtain the skills for this job, how God has provided, what blessings God gives through this provision—a place to live, electricity, and so on.

You can expand on the roles of people who work outside our home—think of all the people who benefit us by their labor: trash collectors, the person in the doctor's office who explains insurance, the mechanic, the hair stylist, book publishers and illustrators, servers in restaurants, and so on. Children could choose a couple and write a note of appreciation.

We parents can call or write our own parents. Such a call would make their day!

Our tradition for Labor Day is to get together with friends for an outdoor barbeque for a great time of fellowship and sharing prayer requests. Such a gathering could be especially significant if friends without employment would be surrounded and prayed for at that time.

NOTE

1. James Winship, *Discipleship Journal*, Issue 115, 2000, 39.

# PRACTICAL Help 22
## Labor Day Quiz

All of the answers for this quiz can be found within this chapter.

1. When is Labor Day celebrated?
2. When was it declared a national holiday?
3. How many states observe it as a legal holiday?
4. What work of God does the Bible describe in its beginning pages?
5. What is the most important work Jesus Christ did?
6. Where did Jesus spend most of His time on earth?
7. What work is God doing today?
8. When did work become a part of God's plan for man?
9. What did the entrance of sin into the world do to work?
10. What is the consequence of an able-bodied man refusing to work and provide for his family?
11. What is to be the motivation for a believer's work, or for whom do we work?
12. What does it mean to work in the name of Jesus?
13. What weekly practice does God give to regulate a person's work from being an idol or too big of a burden?
14. Is there a reward for work beyond this life?
15. Will we work in heaven?

# PRACTICAL Help 23

## Other Ideas for Labor Day Celebration

- Ask God to give you His viewpoint for your job and the grace to do it for Him. Particularly helpful is to visualize God as your boss.

- Have a special time of consecration to present every part of your body to God and the days of your life to Him to fulfill His purposes (Romans 6:12–13; 12:1–2; cf. John 17:4).

- Take time to pray for your employer and for your fellow workers.

- If you have children, take time with them to pray for their present and/or future jobs and employers.

Chapter
Twenty-Seven

Halloween:
*Looking at It
from God's
Perspective*

I read one website that spoke of Halloween as the "best holiday of the year." It was described as a holiday that "produces no stress, leads to no holiday depression afterward, and is just absolutely fun." In regard to spending, it is second only to Christmas. Americans spend over two and half billion dollars a year on Halloween costumes, candy, decorations, and party goods.[1]

## HOW DID IT START?

The roots of this holiday can be traced to the ancient Druids in France, Germany, Britain, and other Celtic countries. The celebration honored the lord of the darkness, their death god, Samhain. November 1 was New Year's Day in their calendar, and the celebration began on October 31 and lasted into the next day. They believed that the spirits of all who died roamed the earth on this evil night and returned to their former home to visit the living. Some believed the evil spirits would "trick" the living if they did not get a "treat."

Before Christianity was introduced to these lands, this celebration of death was not called Halloween. "All Hallows Eve" originated from the pagan holiday honoring the dead. It was an evening to honor all the saints of church history. A "saint" in Roman Catholic theology is one who has earned extra merit, and people can pray to God through them. The concept of "saint" in the Bible is that every Christian is a saint, and Christ alone is our mediator.

Some church historians believe that Pope Gregory IV changed the original May 13 date of All Hallows Eve to make it coincide and counteract the Feast of Samhain, the lord of darkness and god of the dead. All Soul's Day is celebrated after All Saint's Day and is a time to pray for the souls of the dead.

The word "Halloween" is a form of the phrase "All Hallows Eve." Pagan beliefs mixed with medieval superstitions come together to form the background of Halloween that the Irish brought to America.

How should a believer in Christ celebrate Halloween? The answer needs to take into consideration the darkness and superstitious practices that are the background of this holiday. Looking at a calendar of events of the church of Satan a number of years ago revealed that the time around Halloween was a highlight celebration for them. However one chooses to celebrate Halloween, it would be wise for a believer in Christ to use it as an occasion to learn a true Christian perspective of good and evil.

## KNOWING THE SCHEME OF SATAN

A believer in Christ is in a spiritual battle against a well-organized host of angelic beings who have rebelled against God the Creator. As a result, it is necessary to depend on God's strength (Ephesians 6:10–12). Furthermore, the believer is instructed to be informed of our enemy's scheme (2 Corinthians 2:11).

The following verses are a sample of some of the specific works of Satan and his demonic forces. I have found it important to note also what God desires to do and to emphasize that He alone is all powerful.

In regard to the last scheme, child sacrifice was often described with idolatry. The Bible speaks of demonic activity behind idolatry. Even today when one embraces an idol in their life—a hobby, job, etc.—one will sacrifice the spiritual well-being of their children to this idol.

You can add many other schemes of the devil. I am simply suggesting to use this holiday as an occasion to expose the schemes of the evil one against you and your loved ones.

## REALIZING THE INFLUENCE OF THE ENEMY

Satan works in the area of our thinking. There is a great battle in our minds. He seeks to get us to believe a lie and then become preoccupied and controlled by it. As we separately yield to this wrong thought, a habit develops, and this is what some refer to as a stronghold.

The following is a list that may be helpful to use to discern any influence of the evil one.

|  | Satan | All-Powerful God |
|---|---|---|
| Acts 5:3<br>I Timothy 4:1 | Satan tempts to lie and deceive. | God seeks to make us men and women of truth. |
| I Corinthians 7:5 | Satan tempts us to immorality. | God seeks to make us men and women of moral integrity. |
| Revelation 12:4–10 | Satan accuses and slanders us and promotes this attitude in our relationships. | God seeks to affirm, lovingly convict, and promote speech characterized by love. |
| Genesis 3:1–5 | Satan promotes doubt in God's character and His Word. | God seeks to empower us to believe Him and His Word. |
| I Samuel 15:23;<br>I Timothy 3:6 | Satan promotes pride and selfishness. | God promotes humility. |
| I Chronicles 21:1–8;<br>Matthew 16:21–23 | Satan encourages reliance on human resource and human wisdom. | God promotes full confidence in God's perfect power and wisdom. |
| Daniel 7:25 | Satan seeks to "wear out the saints." (This verse is speaking of the Antichrist whom Satan empowers.) | God leads us to true rest and refreshment. |
| Ephesians 4:26–27 | Satan seeks to stir up anger in order to gain an advantage for spiritual, emotional, and physical harm. | God comforts our heart and promotes love and forgiveness. |
| John 13:12; Acts 5:3 | Satan puts wicked purposes into people's minds and hearts. | God puts loving purposes into our minds and hearts. |
| Deuteronomy 18:10 | Satan seeks to harm innocent children. | God welcomes children to love and perfect them. |

- Extreme mood swings
- Repeated night terrors
- Addictions
- Compulsive behavior
- Isolation from family and others
- Occult activities
- Continued fantasizing
- Extreme negative self-image
- Recurring destructive thoughts
- Abuse of the body
- Increasingly rebellious

To be sure we all have a rebellious nature and we cannot abdicate personal responsibility. On the other hand, we should not ignore the influence of the evil one.

## Reclaiming Surrendered Ground

Ask your heavenly Father to let you know of any occultist practice or false teaching with which you may have knowingly or even unknowingly been involved. As you confess any such participation and accept His gracious cleansing, make a decisive break with this involvement (see Acts 19:18–20).

On this holiday ask God to illuminate your inner self in regard to the truth of the person and work of Christ. You might look at the following passages that show Christ's victorious work and authority over the devil and his evil angelic spirits that are called demons.

- John 12:31; 16:11; 17:15
- Ephesians 1:19-23; 2:6; 6:10–18
- Colossians 2:14–15
- 2 Thessalonians 3:3
- Hebrews 2:14–15
- James 4:7
- 1 Peter 6:9

- 1 John 3:8; 4:4
- Revelation 12:10–11

Let this season be an opportunity for appropriate self-examination. List anyone that you have any bitterness toward. In Jesus' love and strength, as an act of your will, offer forgiveness to this one and ask God to use you as an instrument of blessing in their life. Bitterness is probably the most common way we open our lives to the influence of the devil (Ephesians 4:26–27). Let one of your goals for this day be to put your head on the pillow of your bed that night with a clear conscience. As far as it depends on you be at peace with everyone (Romans 12:18).

## HAVE A JOYOUS ALTERNATIVE

If you do not feel free to participate in some of the cultural expressions of this holiday due to its evil heritage, let me suggest that you come up with some alternatives. On this holiday and in all your life "walk in the light" (1 John 1:7), and "do not participate in the unfruitful deal of darkness but instead even expose them" (Ephesians 5:11).

## PENNY'S Thoughts

One alternative to Halloween we have so appreciated was a Fun Fair that one of the local churches has put together in our area. It includes food, contests, games, pony rides, face painting, inflatable jumping structures, and most important, an appropriate gospel witness. Each year the decorations, games, animals, and original play telling the gospel message was centered around a different theme. It was a great outreach to the community and truly a labor of love.

NOTE:
1. holidayinsights.com

# PRACTICAL Help 24

## Other Ideas for Halloween Celebration

- Trunk or Treat—this is an increasingly popular activity for churches. People volunteer to decorate their cars and give out treats from the church parking lot. It's a great alternative to door-to-door and a good witness to the neighborhood.

- Some churches expand Trunk or Treat with costume contests and other games: bobbing for apples, cake walk, ring toss.

- Guests to your home or church party dress up in creative biblical costumes: the pharaoh's daughter, animals on the ark, Roman soldier, shepherds.

- Biblical themes: This is a little different than a biblical characters costume theme. See how creative you can be coming to the party as the fruits of the Spirit; an illustration of a parable (the woman who lost a piece of silver—wear a long dress, carry a broom, candle, coin purse); being a Good Samaritan; faith as small as a mustard seed. One man came to his church's party in his regular clothing and said he was "just as I am." Pa in Laura Ingalls Wilder's book *Little Town on the Prairie* placed two ordinary potatoes on his axe and said it was "commentators on the Acts." Any ideas for dressing as "Peace like a river"?

- Another theme idea: Dress as a Christian hero, historic figure, or martyr.

- Some families celebrate Reformation Day as an alternate to Halloween. You might also learn about and commemorate the Feast of Tabernacles, a Jewish festival celebrated in the fall. Or the Jewish Feast of Purim, which isn't a fall holiday, but it's one when children dress up in costumes.

- Make a homemade tract sharing your own personal testimony, or find an appropriate tract for you or your family to use in your neighborhood. As the trick-or-treaters come to the door, hand the tract out with the candy.

- One family handed out treats at the bus stop in front of their urban home, including a Bible verse with each one.

- Visit a pumpkin patch or go apple picking.

- Be the neighbor who gives out the best/biggest candy (instead of the curmudgeon whose house the kids are afraid of).

- Make it a point of conversation with your kids to talk about what types of costumes are appropriate.

- Go for the "harvest" decorating theme instead of the creepy spider webs and gravestones theme.

- Young children at home or at a church party will enjoy a candy hunt, similar to an Easter egg hunt—don't make it too hard!

- As an alternative to door-to-door trick-or-treating, organize a progressive event with other families. Children can have hot dogs at one home, play games at the next one or more, eat dessert at the last.

- Another alternative to door-to-door is a block party. Your town or neighborhood will have guidelines on how to do this, and in some areas will help by providing an inflatable bouncer and beverages.

- Plan a Noah's Ark party. You can provide material to make costumes on the spot for young children, and older children will enjoy helping—fleece, fabric paint, face paint.

- The youth group can sponsor a pumpkin-related fund-raiser over a couple of weeks: sell pumpkins through a pumpkin patch, run a pumpkin-carving contest, a pumpkin bake-off (enlist the local newspaper to generate interest), hold a pumpkin-carving demonstration, a pumpkin bake sale.

- Make pumpkin bread to give as a love gift. Save the seeds and roast them in a warm oven.

- Too much candy? Freeze some of it in plastic bags and save it for Christmas stockings.

- Make the Halloween season a time to pray for the people closest to you in your life who might be going through hard times.

Much has been said and written about the Christian's response to the secular aspect of Halloween. We can shut our doors and close ourselves off from others, or we can take advantage of the excitement of this holiday to take people a step closer to Christ. As Ephesians 5:15–16 (NLT) says, "Be careful how you live. Don't live like fools, but like those who are wise. Make the most of every opportunity in these evil days." After all, we should not "be overcome by evil, but overcome evil with good" (Romans 12:21).

# A Final Word of Encouragement

What a privilege we have in our wonderful country to be able to include and honor God in each of our celebrations! In this post-modern world the "landscape" is changing rapidly, which is all the more reason to honor the Lord and glorify Him in our holidays and bring our friends, family, the needy, and strangers with us.

We pray that the suggestions in this book do not create any pressure or expectation for you, but only serve as a springboard to the good works God has ordained for you. Let our wonderful Lord meet you in your unique situation and unique circumstance for that day. May you feel wonderfully understood by the Lord in your struggles and may you sense His support as you seek to honor Him.

Would you join us as we prayerfully bring the next holiday on our calendar to the Lord asking Him for His wisdom, His blessing, His agenda in expanding and strengthening His kingdom? If you would like to share your ideas, go to our website www.VictoriousPraying.com and enter your suggestions so that others can be stimulated and aided by your thoughts. As long as we have opportunity, let us encourage one another and stimulate each other to remember our wonderful Lord Jesus in all of life (Hebrews 3:13; 10:24–25).

May God fight your battles and truly bless your holidays.

# Acknowledgments

We would like to acknowledge our debt to the Lord, who has given us true meaning and purpose to our holidays and also His merciful provision of our family and friends.

We are grateful to Greg Thornton for his support in this book and the capable help of Randall Payleitner and Carolyn Shaw and the entire Moody Publishers team. Pam Pugh carefully edited the manuscript and made many helpful suggestions. Ee-Boon Tan, Amanda Lewis, and Scott Wolfe assisted in typing the manuscript. We are grateful for my colleagues and students and many other people who support us in prayer in our ministry.

# A JOURNEY TO VICTORIOUS PRAYING
## STUDY GUIDE AND DVD

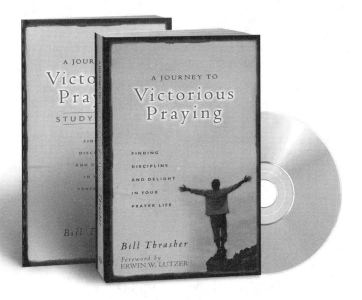

ISBN-13: 978-0-8024-3697-9    ISBN-13: 978-0-8024-3698-6    ISBN-13: 978-0-8024-3694-8

Why do so many people struggle with the discipline and delight of prayer? Dr. Bill Thrasher believes we suffer from fear and a lack of understanding about the nature of prayer. In *A Journey to Victorious Praying*, he teaches readers that prayer is simply coming before Christ with an attitude of helplessness, opening up our needy lives to Him. Filled with practical insight, this book will give readers renewed enthusiasm for embarking on this essential journey.

## MOODY
### PUBLISHERS

moodypublishers.com

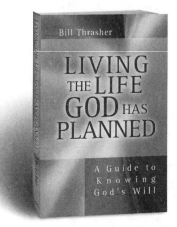

## LIVING THE LIFE GOD HAS PLANNED

"How do I know what God's will is for my life?" It is perhaps the most common question asked by Christians today. Dr. Bill Thrasher teaches readers that they must first seek to know God on a more intimate level before His will becomes more apparent to them. Readers of all maturity levels will appreciate the simplicity and practical nature of this book.

ISBN-13: 978-0-8024-3699-3

## BELIEVING GOD FOR HIS BEST

*Believing God for His Best* is a personal story that will walk you through the author's journey through singleness, and toward marriage. The anecdotal style, coupled with godly wisdom, will inspire singles to trust God for His best.

ISBN-13: 978-0-8024-5573-4

# MOODY
PUBLISHERS

moodypublishers.com